Dead People Have Interesting Things to Say

Randy Ervin

ISBN: 978-0-578-75824-4

Also by Randy Ervin:

Maycroft from 232nd, a novel

An Ordinary Day
The Story of Trooper Layton Davis

What Goes Around…, a novel

Famous Cops You Never Heard Of

Let's Stop Growing Turnips
A Discussion About Gun Violence in America

Foreword

Several years ago I was in Dodge Grove cemetery and happened across the tombstone of a sailor who had died in the Battle of Java Sea. Most WWII buffs will be familiar with the battle as it was, I learned later, a major naval battle. However, when I first saw that grave I had never heard of it. I was struck by the fact that I was standing next to the final resting place of a hero who gave his life in war and I had never heard of the individual or the battle he died in. I wondered how many other stories there might be scattered throughout not only Dodge Grove, but all cemeteries in my hometown. I thought at the time I would like to walk the entire cemetery some day and take note of other interesting things I might see written on headstones. I told myself that someday I would do it and record what I found in a book.

October 17, 2019, was the beginning of that journey. It was a nice day and this project had been on my mind. I grabbed a notebook and pen and a camera, also known as an iPhone, and headed to Dodge Grove Cemetery. I walked through a couple of sections, up and down rows, looking at tombstones. When I saw one that had something interesting written on it, I made some notes and took a picture. I went back a few more times that fall, walking a section or two as time allowed. I never wanted to hurry. I enjoyed these walks. Call it morbid curiosity, but I was fascinated with the stories I found. I also wanted to be respectful, never seeing the task as something I needed to rush through to "get it over with". Winter came and I was maybe half done with Dodge Grove. In April, the weather broke and I was back at it.

On June 1, 2020, I finished walking Dodge Grove and began in Calvary Cemetery. My goal was to walk through all of the main cemeteries in Mattoon: Dodge Grove, Calvary and Resthaven. I finished the last of these cemeteries on July 8, 2020. Then came the real work: sitting down at a computer scouring the archives of old newspaper articles and internet websites trying to find the stories behind the people. Then of course the task was to sift through those articles, piece the stories together and put them down on paper. Or on a hard drive as it were.

Initially I wanted to do something to document/honor all veterans. All too soon I realized there are just too many of them to do that, so I revised my objective. I decided that I would tell the full story of any veteran who either died in combat or who had been a prisoner of war. There are stories here of veterans who died in every war from the Civil War to the wars in Iraq and Afghanistan. I also decided to dedicate a section to display a picture of the tombstone of any veteran who either served in multiple wars or earned multiple medals. Those folks had obviously gone way above and beyond, and they deserve at least a shout out.

I had one concern early on, and I still do. Along the way I have no doubt I missed someone. Some veterans had something written on the back of their tombstone but not the front. There were occasions when I was walking down a row and just happened to turn around and see something on the back of a stone I had already looked at. I also tried to be mindful of time frames of various wars. If a veteran's stone reads "killed in action in France during WWI," that's a pretty good clue. However, many veterans have no such inscription. So if a veteran was 20 years old and he died in 1943, I assumed he was killed in WWII. If he died in 1950 or 1969, I would assume Korea or Vietnam.

Obviously, most of those assumptions were true but not all. I know there are bound to be some veterans whom I just plain missed. I didn't catch the year of death, or I simply missed something I should have seen. For those occasions I am truly sorry and mean no disrespect. My greatest concern with this project is that someone will read this book and say, "My grandfather was killed in Korea, but he isn't in here," or, "My dad was killed in Vietnam but there's nothing about him." I am an army veteran, and I have nothing but respect for all who have worn the uniform but especially for those who served in war. I would never intentionally leave out anyone's story, and if I missed any it was a mistake on my part that I am truly sorry for.

Another thing I want to mention up front is that there was often wording in newspaper articles decades ago that is considered offensive today. On some occasions I have used wording from old newspaper articles verbatim to show how things were reported at the time. My intention is not to cause offense. Therefore, if you read something about a ship being bombed by "a Jap sub" or about someone described as "a colored person", that wording is used only to provide historical context.

Another thing that struck me is how much, or how little, information is on various tombstones, and that if something isn't mentioned then years and decades later the story won't be known. I've written here about a man whose stone says he was the first person to spread word of Lincoln's assassination via the Pony Express and of a man who is a great-great-great grandson of President Zachary Taylor. I would have walked by their graves having no idea how interesting their stories are if they weren't mentioned on their tombstone. Likewise, reading tombstones led me to find the stories about a woman who served five terms on the Raleigh, North Carolina, city council, a man who won a Pulitzer prize and a man who fought in the Battle of the Bulge. I can't help but wonder how many fascinating stories are literally buried in area cemeteries and will never be known because nothing was engraved on a stone.

Something that is as interesting to me as the grave sites is the monuments scattered around the various cemeteries. Dodge Grove in particular has a number of very old monuments. Anyone who has driven or walked through there has seen them, but I wonder how many people know what they are all for, when they were erected and by whom. In addition to the many interesting graves I discovered, I also decided to research all of the monuments and write about them. The history of the monuments is very interesting.

Probably the one thing that struck me as I navigated this journey is just how finite we all are. I saw many stones from the late 1800s and early 1900s that say, "Gone but not forgotten." This will sound harsh, but those words simply aren't true. We will all die one day, and there will be people left behind who remember us. But eventually each and everyone of them will die too and we will be forgotten. So, it isn't nearly as important how, or even if, we are remembered as how we live our lives in the here and now. A hundred years from now you will be just another random plot in the cemetery, with no more importance than anyone else who is alive today regardless of whether you are rich or poor, or whether you are the most popular person in town or completely unknown. But today your life does matter, so make it count. Be a good parent, spouse, friend or neighbor. Bring meaning and joy to someone. Inspire someone. Don't take for granted what a blessing an ordinary day is.

It's been fun seeing ways people are remembered. Some folks have things related to what they loved engraved on their tombstone. I saw engravings of cars, trucks, wildlife, musical notes, sewing machines, trains, and emblems for the Cubs, Cardinals, White Sox and Dodgers. I've also seen things people leave at the grave of their loved ones that are reminders of things that person enjoyed. I've seen whiskey bottles, beer cans, fishing poles, golf balls, marbles and game pieces. I imagine someone on occasion sitting next to the grave of a friend, brother or co-worker, drinking a beer with them, remembering times doing the same in the living room or out on the deck. Then leaving the empty bottle for them. Or of someone leaving a rod or lure on Grandpa's grave remembering all the fishing trips they used to take to the lake. And how what was important wasn't the beer or the fish but the company, conversation and friendship.

I hope you enjoy reading these stories as much as I've enjoyed telling them. I'm glad to know that many of the people whose stories are told here will be remembered. The war heroes deserve to be remembered. Citizens should know who they were and what they did. Likewise, people who died prematurely in fires, train wrecks and other disasters deserve to be remembered. As the saying goes, sit back, relax and enjoy the show. Dead people have interesting things to say.

Dodge Grove Cemetery

On April 7, 1862, a resolution was adopted by the Mattoon City Council to purchase ground for a city cemetery. In December of that year it was given the name Dodge Grove. It formally opened in the spring of 1863. According to William LeBaron, Jr. in *The History of Coles County, Illinois*, Dodge Grove received its name as a result of a horse race in Springfield, Illinois. The Whitley family, owners of the "Dodge Filly," had staked their mare in a race and lost. Not wanting to lose the horse, they returned home and turned the horse loose in a grove of trees. The new owner and officers of the law could not find the mare in the grove, and "thus the filly dodged capture and the grove captured the name of Dodge." Francis Ada Robertson, who died at the age of three years and 11 months, was the first person buried in the cemetery on March 20, 1863.

William D. Haskell
1916-1942

Lost In Battle Of Java Sea

William Haskell is the person who started this journey of mine. I mentioned in the forward how I had come across the grave of a war hero in Dodge Grove cemetery and wondered how many other interesting stories might be waiting to be discovered. Well, Mr. Haskell is that hero. As I stated earlier, I had never heard of the Battle of Java Sea. Here's a little information about it; then I will tell you what I learned about Mr. Haskell's journey.

The Battle of the Java Sea was a decisive naval battle of the Pacific campaign of World War II. Allied navies suffered a disastrous defeat at the hand of the Imperial Japanese Navy on February 27, 1942, and in secondary actions over successive days. The aftermath of the battle included several smaller actions around Java, including the smaller but also significant Battle of Sunda Strait. These defeats led to Japanese occupation of the entire Dutch East Indies.

On January 23, 1942, a force of four American destroyers attacked a Japanese invasion convoy in Makassar Strait as it approached Balikpapan in Borneo. On February 13, the Allies fought unsuccessfully in the Battle of Palembang, to prevent the Japanese from capturing the major oil port in eastern Sumatra. On the night of February 19 an Allied force attacked the Eastern Invasion Force off Bali in the Battle of Badung Strait. Also on February 19 the Japanese made two air raids on Darwin on the Australian mainland, one from carrier-based planes and the other by land-based planes. The destruction of Darwin rendered it useless as a supply and naval base to support operations in the East Indies.

The Allied force engaged the Japanese in the Java Sea, and the battle raged intermittently from mid-afternoon to midnight as the Allies tried to reach and attack the troop transports of the Java invasion fleet, but they were repulsed by superior firepower. The Allies had local air superiority during the daylight hours because Japanese air power could not reach the fleet in the bad weather. The weather also hindered communications, making cooperation between the many

2

Allied parties involved even worse than it already was. The Japanese also jammed the radio frequencies. *Exeter* was the only ship in the battle equipped with radar, an emerging technology at the time. The battle consisted of a series of attempts to reach and attack the invasion convoy; each was rebuffed by the escort force with heavy losses being inflicted on the Allies. The fleets sighted each other at about 4:00 pm on February 27 and closed to firing range, opening fire at 4:16.

Both sides exhibited poor gunnery and torpedo skills during this phase of the battle. *Exeter's* shells did not come close to the Japanese ships, while *Houston* only managed to achieve a straddle on one of the opposing cruisers. The only notable result of the initial gunnery exchange was *Exeter* being critically damaged by a hit in the boiler room from an 8-inch shell. The ship then limped away. The Japanese launched two huge torpedo salvoes, consisting of 92 torpedoes in all, but scored only one hit, on *Kortenaer*. She was struck by a Long Lance, broke in two and sank rapidly after the hit. *Electra*, covering *Exeter*, engaged in a duel with *Jintsū* and *Asagumo*, scoring several hits but suffering severe damage. After a serious fire started on *Electra* and her remaining turret ran out of ammunition, abandon ship was ordered. On the Japanese side, only *Asagumo* was forced to retire because of damage.

The Allied fleet broke off and turned away around 6:00, covered by a smoke screen laid by the four destroyers of U.S Destroyer Division 58 (DesDiv 58). They also launched a torpedo attack but at too long a range to be effective. Dutch Naval Commander Karel Doorman's force turned south toward the Java coast, then west and north as night fell in an attempt to evade the Japanese escort group and fall on the convoy. It was at this point the ships of DesDiv 58, their torpedoes expended, left on their own initiative to return to Surabaya. Shortly after, at 9:25, *Jupiter* ran onto a mine and was sunk, while about 20 minutes later, the fleet passed where *Kortenaer* had sunk earlier, and *Encounter* was detached to pick up survivors.

Doorman's command, now reduced to four cruisers, again encountered the Japanese escort group at 11:00; both columns exchanged fire in the darkness at long range, until *De Ruyter* and *Java* were sunk by one devastating torpedo salvo. Doorman and most of his crew went down with *De Ruyter*; only 111 were saved from both ships. Only the cruisers *Perth* and *Houston* remained; low on fuel and ammunition, and following Doorman's last instructions, the two ships retired, arriving at Tanjung Priok on 28 February.

Perth and *Houston* were at Tanjung Priok on February 28 when they received orders to sail through Sunda Strait to Tjilatjap. Material was running short in Java, and neither was able to rearm or fully refuel. Departing at 7:00 pm on February 28 for the Sunda Strait, by chance they encountered the main Japanese invasion fleet for West Java in Bantam Bay. The Allied ships were engaged by at least three cruisers and several destroyers. In a ferocious night action that ended after midnight on March 1, *Perth* and *Houston* were sunk.

The Allied losses during the battle of Java Sea were devastating. Two light cruisers and two destroyers were sunk, and one heavy cruiser was damaged. 2300 Allied sailors were killed compared to only 36 Japanese. This is the story of one of those 2300, William D. Haskell of Mattoon, who was on board the *U.S.S. Houston* when she went down.

A small blurb in the *Journal-Gazette* on October 8, 1940 said: "William Haskell, US Navy, who has been home on a 10 day furlough visiting his parents left today for Mare Island,

CA where he will be assigned to the *U.S.S Houston*. He will then leave for China where he will be stationed for 2.5 years." This was over a year before the attack on Pearl Harbor. While war was raging in Europe between several western European countries and Hitler's Nazi Germany, most Americans couldn't even comprehend the possibility of being involved in the war. It was peace time. I'm sure Mr. Haskell's parents were concerned as any parent would be when their child moves away or joins the military, but there wasn't the heightened concern of war. Little could they have imagined that a year later we would be brought into a world war, and a year after that their son would be on his ship in the middle of the Pacific Ocean fighting for his life.

On March 16, 1942, a story's headline read: "Believed to have perished in great battle for Java." The article reported that "William D. Haskell, son of Mr. and Mrs. Ed Haskell, 620 N. 22nd, is "missing in action" according to a message received by his parents late Saturday from the Navy Department. The message instructed the family not to give any information about Young Haskell's ship. It is known, however, that he had been on the *USS Houston*, a cruiser which the Navy Department announced Saturday was missing and presumed lost in a titanic naval battle off Java on February 27. Local friends presume, therefore, that he was on board the *Houston* when it was lost.

Two young Mattoon men who were reported missing early in the war later were found, and Mattoon residents maintained hope today that young Haskell will be found. Kenneth Gaines was reported missing in the first raid on Hickman Field, HI but later was found. Jack Romans was reported missing by the Navy Department in the same raid but also was accounted for. The ship on which he had been stationed, the *U.S.S Oklahoma*, had been sunk at Pearl Harbor.

Young Haskell was born in Mattoon April 3, 1916. He spent his entire life in Mattoon until he enlisted in the navy March 12, 1940. He has two brothers and two sisters."

On October 26, 1943, the *Journal Gazette* ran an article listing area service members who were listed as Missing in Action. William Haskell was on the list. I can't imagine the agony that must have been for his parents. The waiting, uncertainty and worry. It had been a year and a half since they had received word their son's ship was lost. They probably knew the likelihood of him still being alive was slim, but they wouldn't have given up hope. Imagine your child missing for that long. You receive no information. You're in a constant state of despair.

On September 26, 1945, another article appeared regarding Mr. Haskell. It said his parents were hopeful he was still alive and would be found in a Japanese POW camp. Their daughter, Mrs. J.A. Poliquin of Maryland, talked to three survivors at the naval hospital in Bethesda, MD. The three were rescued from a prison camp in Thailand and flown to the U.S. by way of Calcutta, India. They said they knew William, but he was not interned at their POW camp, but there was a slight chance he may have been picked up by another rescue boat. They said Haskell, a ship's cook third class, was two decks below in the first aid station at the time of the sinking. After their rescue they said they were imprisoned at Java from March to November, then separated. Most of *Houston's* officers were sent to Japan; however, the three with whom she talked were sent to Moulmein, Burma, in 1943 where they took part in the construction of a railroad. From there they were interned in Thailand.

A little less than a month later, on October 18, 1945, the official word came. The paper reported: "William Dale Haskell, 29, who served as a ship's cook third class aboard the cruiser

USS Houston, has been officially declared killed as a result of enemy action on March 1, 1942 according to a telegram received late Wednesday by his parents. Haskell, who was reported missing early in 1942, was believed to have been a victim of the titanic naval battle off Java on February 27, 1942. No word concerning him was received during that time and in August 1945 Mr. and Mrs. Haskell renewed their hopes that he might be one of the 300 survivors of the cruiser who were found in a secret Japanese POW camp."

Three and a half agonizing years after receiving word their son's ship was lost and he was missing in action, the devastating blow was dealt. It was official, Mr. Haskell was in fact a casualty of war.

Dr. Elmer E. Barr.
Beloved husband of Katherine Barr
Born Mattoon, August 24, 1867
Died Los Angeles, April 14, 1901

This headstone struck me for a couple reasons. First, I thought it was interesting to find a doctor from Mattoon who practiced in the nineteenth century. He was born just two years after the end of the Civil War during a time when many people couldn't read and write, let alone graduate high school and go on to study an advanced curriculum like medicine. Second, during an era when long distance travel was not common, how and why did this man end up in Los Angeles? My research uncovered an even more interesting piece of information about him: he was black. I don't know the data on the percentage of doctors who were black in the late 1800s, but it had to be low. I also imagine there weren't many black families in Mattoon, IL during that time.

An article dated December 24, 1896, in a newspaper called the *Inner Ocean* in Chicago was headlined: HONOR TO THEIR RACE. Two Colored Physicians on the Hospital Staff.

They are Drs. Elmer E. Barr and Wilberforce Williams. The article read: "In the recent reorganization of the medical staff of Cook County hospital the colored physicians of Chicago received flattering recognition, two of their number obtaining appointments. They are Dr. Elmer E. Barr and A. Wilberforce Williams. Dr. Barr is among the younger colored professional men in the west but has achieved some distinction as a physician and a man of influence among his people. He is a native of this state having been born in the town of Mattoon in 1867. His education was completed in the schools of his native city.

In 1889 he came to Chicago and entered the Rush medical college, from which place he graduated in 1893 and became house physician at Providence Hospital. After a service of two and a half years he took up the active practice of his profession. He is now a gynecologist on the Provident staff. He is also the president of The Colored Men's Sunday Club and shows an active interest in all matters pertaining to the colored people of Chicago."

So apparently Dr. Barr lived in Mattoon his entire childhood, finishing school here. I wonder what his life and the life of his family were like. Were they accepted? Were they shunned? Did teachers encourage or discourage his interest in medicine? What did his parents do for a living and how and where did they live? I wasn't able to find much in the way of information about him prior to leaving for Chicago to study medicine. Regarding his motive for moving to Los Angeles, that was learned in his obituary which was printed in the *Los Angeles Times* on April 18, 1901. It read: "Dr. Elmer E Barr, a colored physician and surgeon, who died in this city Sunday evening was a man of ability and education who would have been a conspicuous figure among the leaders of his race had consumption not claimed him as a victim. Born in Mattoon, Ill in 1867 the son of Mr. and Mrs. S.C. Barr. He was married in 1885. Two years later with declining health, he moved to Los Angeles hoping to receive benefit from the change. He was able to resume his practice and acquire considerable property, but the germs of disease were too deeply seated to be eradicated. He was a member of Ancient Order of Foresters, The Odd Fellows and The Household of Ruth. He gathered about him many friends wherever he was located and was highly esteemed by all. Funeral services conducted at the Azusa-Street A.M.E. church by Elder Edwards at 1:00 p.m. Thursday. The remains will be sent to Mattoon, accompanied by his wife, mother and five-year-old son."

David W. Allison
Engineer for Big Four Railway Co.
Killed at Wabash Bridge Oct. 28, 1892. Aged 36 yrs. 9 mo. 22 days

It's difficult to imagine that a peaceful stretch of the Wabash River about a mile north of Fairbanks Park was twice the scene of tragedy and tremendous wreckage more than a century ago. The second railroad bridge upstream from Fairbanks Park was known as the Big Four Wabash River Bridge. There, in 1892 and in 1900, massive train accidents caused the deaths of two men and sent three locomotives and dozens of train cars plunging into the river. For several decades, at least one locomotive involved in the crashes remained visible, still in the river, according to Mike McCormick, Vigo County historian. It's believed that the locomotive rests now below the surface of the water near the Big Four Bridge. As many as two other steam engines may also remain under water in the same area.

The drought of 2012 brought the water level of the Wabash to historic lows, revealing many of the river's secrets. With the newly shallow water, area residents have dusted off rumors of an ancient cannon in the river near the former Fort Harrison site, a cache of Civil War-era weapons downstream from Terre Haute and other sunken "treasures." But most interest has been focused on the possibility of uncovering the lost locomotives below the Big Four Bridge. Interested locals have searched the water, but no conclusive proof of the locomotives has been uncovered.

In 1892, a speeding locomotive slammed into a parked engine about midway across the long bridge. The impact sent the speeding engine at least two stories into the air, according to local historians. That accident caused a section of the bridge to collapse and sent both engines

7

and several train cars plunging into the water below. The impact of that terrifying crash "could be heard for a mile," the *Terre Haute Evening Gazette* reported at the time. Engineer David W. "Wes" Allison could not be found amid the wreckage, and his body was not discovered until the following spring. His was the only death in that accident.

Oct. 28, 1892, *Mattoon Gazette*: "David W. Allison, a resident of Mattoon, Ill., was operating an eastbound freight express from St. Louis, hauling cattle and perishable freight. It had been scheduled to arrive in Terre Haute at 1:41 a.m. but was running about five hours behind. The westbound train had arrived at the Terre Haute freight depot at North Fourth Street about 6:30 a.m. to allow a passenger train to pull onto a siding near the North Seventh Street depot. Engineer Jim Flynn edged his vacant train onto the bridge.

Advised that Allison's train No. 42 was expected soon, Flynn dispatched a flagman to the west side of the bridge. Without forewarning, the steam-driven charge emerged from around the bend at about 40 miles per hour. The flag was waved but Allison responded by blowing the whistle. Inexplicably, the brakes did not engage. Quickly realizing it would be impossible for Allison to stop, Flynn tried to back up before jumping from the locomotive and crawling onto a stone pier. He reached safety seconds before the collision. The terrified flagman exited the bridge at its west end.

At the moment of impact the engine on the eastbound stock train leaped at least two stories into the air, knocking Flynn's locomotive backward three car lengths. The sound of the collision was succeeded by the deafening crash of the collapsing bridge, moans and bellows from injured and fearful cattle, hissing steam, smoke and flying debris. Except for Allison, personnel on both trains escaped serious injury. Before evacuating his locomotive as it penetrated the bridge, fireman C.P. South urged Allison to jump, too. Conductor J.P. Sturgeon and one brakeman vaulted from the back of the caboose. Two other caboose members safely remained on board.

Four cars from each train tumbled into the river. A car from each dangled at the break. Four cattle cars were full and several head were crushed or so severely injured that they had to be destroyed. One carload survived, swimming to the riverbank. A refrigerator car full of poultry burst and barrels of chicken floated down river.

Severely injured, engineer Allison disappeared into the murky water soon after his locomotive submerged. Despite prolonged searches by Terre Haute diver John Benz and other rescue personnel, his body was not recovered until April 22, 1893. A steam hoist brought in to clear debris did not work well until the timber was set afire. Nevertheless, partial rail service was restored on Nov. 1."

Webb Ross

Engineer for Big Four Southwestern Limited. Killed at Wann, Ill Jan. 21, 1893 while trying to save his train

Just a few months after the railroad accident that took the life of Mattoon resident David Wes Allison, another train engineer from Mattoon lost his life in a railway accident, this time in Wann, Illinois, a small town near Alton.

The Wann Disaster was a horrific railroad tragedy that occurred in Madison County involving the greatest loss of life in a single incident and the most numerous cases of personal injury in the county's history. It occurred near the Wann Station at Alton Junction (East Alton) on the Big Four Railroad, about 4 miles east of Alton, near the corner of Shamrock and Main in the present-day village of East Alton.

On Saturday, January 21, 1893, the Southwestern Limited train on the Cleveland, Cincinnati, Chicago & St. Louis Railroad (also called the Big Four) left St. Louis at 8:05 am and was due at Wann Station at 8:50 am. Howard Clelland was the Conductor of the five passenger cars drawn by Engine No. 109. The engineer was Webb Ross of Mattoon, and the fireman was Richard White, also of Mattoon.

The train was running at a higher rate of speed than usual, approaching a slight curve. Rounding the curve, Ross instantly saw that a switch was mistakenly left open with a long line of oil tank cars on the track. Fireman White immediately jumped, while Engineer Ross applied the brakes, but it was too late. The passenger train collided with the 25 oil tank cars. Initially, most passengers were not injured in the collision. When the nearby residents and business owners heard

9

the collision, they ran toward the train, some giving aid, some merely watching the spectacle, not knowing what was about to happen.

The oil tankers caught fire from the collision, and a terrible explosion followed, sending 7,000 gallons of burning oil, later called "a rain of fire," fifty feet into the air. Engineer Ross was not injured in the initial collision. He had jumped from the train and was standing safely to the side when burning oil rained down pouring over him, burning him so severely his charred body was unrecognizable. Later, he was picked up and carried to a house. Fireman White stood beside the dead body of his companion moaning and was reported to have said, "He saved the passengers but lost his life in doing it."

The large crowd of spectators that had gathered nearby were literally covered with the burning oil. The scene was terrible. Most were literally charred; others had the flesh burned to the bone. Moans and screams of the wounded filled the air. Five dead bodies were recovered immediately, two boys and three men. One of the boys burned to death was Edward Miller of Alton Junction. His father, William Miller, was very badly burned. Seven more tank cars caught fire and burned. Nearby trees burned. All the houses near the scene were destroyed. Literally thousands of people arrived at the scene to help any way they could. All the doctors from Alton and nearby communities were summoned. The survivors were placed on a Big Four special train and brought to Alton. From the depot they were transported to St. Joseph's Hospital by wagon.

An article in the Alton paper said, "In the southeast ward where the fatally burned ones are confined, a scene calculated to make the heart sad was presented. There are ten victims in this room. Lying on the beds, surrounded each by a few friends, the victims of that seething rain of oil writhe in their agony. Their quivering flesh is wrapped in cotton from their toes to top of their head. Nothing but lips are visible and it is impossible to tell whom you are gazing. Their lips are swollen to an enormous size, and in some instances glued together, requiring water to be sprayed upon them almost constantly. The bodies enveloped in cotton writhe and quiver and the poor victim gasps for breath and moans piteously. The room has a sickening odor. On the first couch lay Joseph Herman, his form in cotton reclining on the arm of a loving father, a weeping sister beside him, unable to speak. The names of the injured are written on a slip of paper and pasted over the top of the bedstead.

In Ward No. 2 are eight more victims, a few of whom are not entirely enveloped in cotton and present awful appearances, a description of which we will not give. In three wards there were twenty-three victims, seven dead removed since the first arrival. As the victims breathe their last, they are taken to the dead room and placed in the hands of undertakers. The bedding at the hospital gave out. A relief committee yesterday purchased large quantities and had it sent to the hospital."

Blame for the accident centered on Albert Gratten, a switchman employed by the Big Four at Wann. Apparently Gratten was a barber by trade and was hired as a switchman not long before when a number of men quit over a wage dispute. He was reported in the newspaper to be a novice and incapable of doing his work properly. The paper initially said he had not been seen since the accident. It was later discovered that he had been burned severely on his head, and had not fled.

A gentleman in Alton who was a witness of the explosion, and who was just out of harm's way, related the following: "As soon as the explosion occurred, everyone seemed paralyzed. A seething rain of fire descended on those that were watching the fire from the little grove on the bank, this side of the conflagration. Immediately men and boys, blazing from head to foot, started to run through the grove. Many dropped before they had gone any distance, and others stopped, frantically trying to remove a coat, vest or shirt. Some were in such agony that they removed every vestige of clothing and ran pell mell to the station. It was an awful sight."

Another witness was standing at a grocery store near the scene. He said, "Just after the stunning report of the explosion, a man rushed toward where several others and myself were standing. He shouted, 'For God's sake, men, cut these boots off of me.' Knives promptly cut the leather from the top to toe. The oil had filled both boots and burned his legs to a crisp. When his boots were taken off, the clothing and flesh came with them. He was in awful agony." The man was fatally burned.

The January 27, 1893, edition of the *Mattoon Gazette* ran a large front page story on the tragedy with the headline: "A Hero's Death. Engineer Webb Ross gives his life that others might be saved." The article said he had been a resident of Mattoon for twenty-four years and had been employed with The Big Four since 1857. A description of the accident read, "A grinding of the airbrakes, the sudden jar of the engine's reversal, a crash, a flood of running fire, a few gasps and struggles-and Webb Ross fell back into the flames. A few hours later a charred and disfigured corpse was brought to his home in this city from whence only a short time ago had gone forth a magnificent specimen of stalwart manhood."

Mr. Ross had served as an alderman on the city council. He was survived by his wife Clara, five sons and a daughter. A child who had died in infancy preceded him in death.

The receiving vault was completed in 1903 and was used for temporary storage of bodies that were not yet ready to be buried for any reason. The contract to build the vault was awarded to S.M. Clark and Company in Mattoon. Today such bodies are kept in a funeral home or in the morgue so there has not been a use for the vault for many years. An article dated August 6, 1903, in the *Mattoon Daily Journal* reported on the first use of the new vault. It read, "The new receiving vault at Dodge Grove cemetery was used for the first time Wednesday. The funeral services of Miss Chapman were held at the new Presbyterian church, and owing to the stormy weather the remains were not interred at the cemetery, but were placed in the receiving vault to be interred later in the family lot at the convenience of the family."

In 1906 the remains of a man killed when he was hit by a train were placed in the receiving vault. The man's identity was not known and the body was placed in the vault while the authorities tried to determine who he was. In 1910 the funeral of Engineer Tim Toole was held, and burial was to be in Calvary Cemetery. The body was placed in the Dodge Grove receiving vault pending the arrival of relatives who were traveling from Colorado. In 1918 the body of Mrs. Oscar Donhost was placed in the receiving vault until her husband could return home from the battlefield in France where he was fighting in WWI. These are but a few of the many stories of the vault's use over the years.

C. Lamont Eldridge Nov. 3, 1879
Harry D. Eldridge Dec. 23, 1887
Lost their lives in the Iroquois Theatre fire at Chicago December 30, 1903

I was intrigued to read this inscription. I had never heard of this fire, and it seemed such a tragedy that two brothers were killed in the disaster. Monte was a 24-year-old railroad worker employed by the Big Four, and Harry was a 17-year-old high school student. An internet search revealed dozens of articles about the tragedy. The Iroquois Theatre was on West Randolph Street between State Street and Dearborn Street in Chicago, and it opened on November 23, 1903. The theater had only one entrance. A broad stairway which led from the foyer to the balcony level was also used to reach the stairs to the gallery level. Theater designers claimed this allowed

13

patrons to "see and be seen" regardless of the price of their seats. However, the common stairway ignored Chicago fire ordinances that required separate stairways and exits for each balcony. The design proved disastrous: people exiting the gallery encountered a crowd leaving the balcony level, and people descending from the upper levels met the orchestra level patrons in the foyer.

On December 30, 1903, a Wednesday, the Iroquois presented a matinee performance of the popular Drury Lane musical *Mr. Blue Beard*, which had been playing at the Iroquois since opening night. The December 30 performance drew a much larger sellout audience. Tickets were sold for every seat in the house, plus hundreds more for the "standing room" areas at the back of the theater. Many of the estimated 2,100–2,200 patrons attending the matinee were children. The standing room areas were so crowded that some patrons sat in the aisles, blocking the exits. At about 3:15 p.m., shortly after the beginning of the second act, sparks from an arc light ignited a muslin curtain, probably as a result of an electrical short circuit. A stagehand tried to douse the fire, but it quickly spread to the fly gallery high above the stage.

Actor Eddie Foy, who was preparing to go on stage at the time, ran out and attempted to calm the crowd, first making sure that his young son was in the care of a stagehand. He later wrote, "It struck me as I looked out over the crowd during the first act that I had never before seen so many women and children in the audience. Even the gallery was full of mothers and children." Foy was widely seen as a hero after the fire for his courage in remaining on stage and pleading with patrons not to panic even as large chunks of burning scenery landed around him.

By this time, many of the patrons on all levels were attempting to flee the theater. Some had found the fire exits hidden behind draperies on the north side of the building, but found that they could not open the locks. Three doors were forced open. Some patrons panicked, crushing or trampling others in a desperate attempt to escape from the fire, and many were killed while trapped in dead ends or while trying to open what looked like doors with windows in them but were actually only windows. Patrons who were able to escape via the emergency exits on the north side found themselves on the unfinished fire escapes. Many jumped or fell from the icy, narrow fire escapes to their deaths; the bodies of the first jumpers broke the falls of those who followed them.

Mass panic ensued and, attempting their own escape from the burning building, many of those trapped inside tried climbing over piles of bodies. The lights went out, adding to the panic as frightened patrons tried to find exits in pitch darkness with smoke rapidly filling the building. Corpses were stacked 10 feet high around some of the blocked exits. The victims were asphyxiated by the fire, smoke, and gases, or were crushed to death by the onrush of other terrified theater patrons behind them. 602 people died in the fire, and hundreds more were injured. The Great Chicago Fire, by comparison, killed about 300 people. After the fire, it was alleged that fire inspectors had been bribed with free tickets to overlook code violations.

The day before the fire, the young men's parents, Mr. and Mrs. George Eldridge (George was a Civil War veteran), saw their sons off at the train depot in Mattoon for a trip to Chicago. Among other activities in the city, the brothers had tickets to see a play at the newly opened Iroquois Theatre. When news of the fire broke, friends and relatives raced to Chicago to try and learn of the brothers' fate while their parents remained at home and waited for news. One can only imagine the agony that wait must have been. There were no cell phones. No internet or 24/7 news stations. Chances are the parents didn't even have a phone in their home. There was no way to track developments except to wait for news to be delivered to them.

Sadly, news of Monte's death came the first day. His body was badly charred, and he appeared to have burned to death. He was identified by personal papers found in one of his pockets. Harry's body on the other hand was not located. Friends scoured hospitals and morgues (hotels, restaurants and even taverns had been turned into makeshift morgues with as many bodies stacked up as those facilities could hold), hoping to locate him and learn his fate. Obviously everyone hoped he had been able to get out of the building and would be found alive in a hospital. Newspaper accounts reported that the grief stricken mother stayed in her bedroom while Mr. Eldridge was seen pacing back and forth on the sidewalk in front of their home for hours on end.

On January 1st, two agonizing days after the fire, hope was dashed for the parents when Harry's body was found. Like his brother, his body was badly charred, but cause of death was determined to have been a result of being trampled to death after falling to the floor and being overrun by stampeding patrons. Harry was identified by clothing and some personal effects that were on his person and identified by his parents.

The *Mattoon Daily Journal* January 9, 1904, edition reported the funeral for the brothers was the largest the city had ever seen. Long before the service began, the Methodist church was already filled with scores of people standing at the back of the sanctuary and in the aisles while others stood outside in the cold. The funeral was conducted by Rev. J.B. Horney and Rev. Naboth Osborne. Rev. Horney recounted how the boys had waved to their parents at the depot as their train departed and said, "We'll be home again in a day or two." Sobs filled the air. Two hearses waited outside the church, a black one for Monte and a white one for Harry, to transport their remains to the cemetery.

The newspaper article about the funeral summed up this way: "It will be a long time before Mattoon recovers from the pall of sadness that is hanging over her on account of the terrible death of these two young men, and their memory will long live in the hearts of those who knew them."

Lieutenant Richard L. Morgan 1931-1954

God bless my plane. I ask God's blessings on my plane as I set forth each day. I let his hand rest on the stick because he knows the way. For every journey that I take it matters not how far. Over the mountains the plains and the waters, my Father runs my plane. Though storms may come and darkness fall I never lose the track. The God who sends me forth each day will bring me safely back.

Twenty-two-year-old Second Lieutenant Richard Morgan was a military pilot. He was killed instantly when the T-33 jet trainer plane he was flying crashed and exploded east of Waco, Texas. The January 13, 1954 edition of the *Journal Gazette* reported that the American Legion conducted military burial rites for Lt. Morgan at the Presbyterian church and Dodge Grove cemetery. The article lists him as a nephew of Mr. and Mrs. Dale Hill of Mattoon. No other family members are listed.

Dr. Doran Therman Rue, M.D. and Mildred Chambers Rue, R.N.

A husband and wife; one a doctor, the other a nurse. Both died in 1939 in their 30s. Obviously I thought it was interesting that the couple were both medical professionals. Given their young age, and the fact they appeared to have died at the same time, I wondered what might have happened. Had they been killed in a car accident? Could it have been a fire, tornado or other disaster? Some research revealed a strange, and sad, ending for the couple.

The headline in the *Journal Gazette* on March 31, 1939, read "Mattoon Doctor and Wife Found Dead." The article told of the discovery of the bodies in what was apparently a double suicide. The couple were found dead in bed in a cabin at Lithia Springs that was owned by Dr. Rue's brother W.E. Rue. The bodies were discovered by Amos Woods, a caretaker at the property. The cause of death was stated to be an overdose of a sleep-inducing drug called Nembutal. A bottle of the drug and a syringe were found on a table by the bed. A.J. Bridges, owner of Bridges East Side drug store, reported that Mrs. Rue purchased a bottle of Nembutal about 10:00 pm the previous evening. He said she talked freely and appeared in good spirits. Relatives could give no motive for suicide but did note Dr. Rue had been in poor health for several years.

Dr. Rue was born and raised in Mattoon. He was a graduate of Mattoon High School and the University of Illinois school of medicine. The newspaper article said he was an outstanding athlete, having starred on the Mattoon and U of I track teams. He was the captain of the track team at Illinois his senior year. The couple had been married three years and had no children. Dr. Rue was survived by his parents of Mattoon and three siblings. No information was given about Mrs. Rue, so perhaps she was not from the area.

Miscellaneous articles revealed that Dr. Rue practiced as a physician for a period of time at Saint Luke's hospital in Chicago as late as 1934. A 1938 article places him back in Mattoon where he testified at the coroner's inquest of a man who had been killed in a hunting accident.

Dr. Rue had performed the autopsy. In February 1939, a month before the suicides, Dr. Rue moved his offices into a renovated space in a building located at 1500 Wabash Ave.

A double funeral was held Sunday, April 2, at 2:00 pm at Schilling Funeral Home in Mattoon with Rev. Horace Batchelor officiating. Six local physicians served as pallbearers.

Memorial near veteran's drive: T.O.T.E. Dowagiac Tribe 260 G.S.D. 414.

This memorial (front and back pictured) stands alone toward the north portion of the cemetery near Veteran's Drive. I wondered how many people have seen it and have no idea what it means. I must admit you can put me in that category. T.O.T.E. is a secret password of an organization known as the Improved Order of Red Men (I.O.R.M.), that was originally intended to be known only to members. It stands for "Totem of the Eagle."

The IORM claims to be the oldest of the secret societies in America. The claim is based on its evolution from earlier organizations founded even before the American Revolution including the Sons of Liberty and the Sons of Tamina. They claim that the Sons of Liberty worked underground in Colonial times to establish freedom and liberty. As known now, the IORM was founded in 1834 and was organized as the Great Council of the United States by 1847, with headquarters in Baltimore, Maryland. At its peak in 1921, there were 519,942 members in forty-six states. In 1978 its membership was 31,789.

The IORM secret ritual, like many others, shows Masonic influence. Its three basic degrees are Adoption, Warrior and Chief. A fourth degree is related to Insurance Beneficiary elements. Local lodges are called "Tribes." Non-members are called "Paleface." A meeting site is a "Wigwam." It was closed to non-whites until 1974 when its 106th session of the Great Council eliminated the racial requirement. The IORM has become active in support of American Indian Development programs designed to aid in education and health of Native American children.

The Pokagon Band of Potawatomi Indians is a federally recognized Potawatomi-speaking tribe based in southwestern Michigan and northeastern Indiana. Tribal government functions are located in Dowagiac, Michigan. The tribal membership was approximately 4,990 members as of

2014. They occupy reservation lands in a total of ten counties in the area. I assume someone connected with the tribe in Dowagiac, MI was responsible for the placement of this memorial since it bears that tribe's name, but I could find no information about this specific memorial to include who was responsible for placing it here. At any rate, if you have occasion to see this memorial you now know what TOTE means, and you have a little understanding of the history of the Dowagiac Tribe it mentions.

Curtis E. Troth
Oct. 25, 1867-Aug. 8, 1921
I.C. Brakeman killed at Macon Ill

Curtis E. "Curl" Troth was a 53-year-old resident of Clinton, IL and had formerly lived in Mattoon at 821 Wabash Ave. where he operated a store out of the back of his house. He was a brakeman on the Illinois Central Railroad. He was walking on top of a train, lost his footing, and fell. Presumably he fell onto the track and was run over, but the newspaper article did not say specifically how he died so that is only conjecture. The accident happened at 1:30 pm near Macon, IL.

Cpl. Rosamond L. Reed, Pvt. and Lawrence C. Reed
130 Inf. A.E.F. (American Expeditionary Forces)
Killed in Action in France during WWI

Both soldiers, not related, died within days of each other fighting in France during WWI- Rosamond in the Meuse-Argonne Offensive and Lawrence in the Argonne Forest. A joint funeral was held in Mattoon nearly three years later on August 21, 1921.

The Meuse-Argonne offensive was a major part of the final Allied offensive of World War I that stretched along the entire Western Front. It was fought from September 26, 1918, until the Armistice of November 11, 1918, a total of 47 days. The Meuse-Argonne offensive was the largest in United States military history, involving 1.2 million American soldiers. It is the second deadliest battle in American history, resulting in over 350,000 casualties including 28,000 German lives, 26,277 American lives and an unknown number of French lives. U.S. losses were worsened by the inexperience of many of the troops, the tactics used during the early phases of the operation, and the widespread onset of the global influenza outbreak called the "Spanish Flu". Meuse-Argonne was the principal engagement of the American Expeditionary Force (AEF) during World War I. It was one of a series of Allied attacks known as the Hundred Days Offensive, which brought the war to an end. It was the largest and bloodiest operation of World War I for the AEF. During the Meuse-Argonne offensive several United States Army soldiers earned the Medal of Honor, including Sergeant Alvin C. York.

The Forest of Argonne is a long strip of rocky mountain and wild woodland in north-eastern France, approximately 120 miles east of Paris. During World War I, the forest was the site of intense military action. Bitter fighting between German and Allied units took place there in autumn and winter 1914, summer 1915 and autumn 1918.

Funeral services for the fallen heroes were held at the Methodist Episcopal church. Rev. R.F. McDaniel delivered the sermon for Rosamond with the theme "I have fought a good fight". He spoke of the nobleness of spirit that causes one to sacrifice his life for his country. Rev. J.F. McMahan, speaking on a theme of "Greater love hath no man but this, that he lay down his life for his friends", delivered the sermon for Lawrence.

One hundred forty-two veterans paid their respects by marching in a double column from the church to the cemetery. The firing squad fired a separate salute over each grave. It was estimated that over 1000 people attended the funeral.

Lawrence Reed was survived by his father, Jack, of 3200 Marshall Ave. His mother was killed in the 1917 tornado. Lawrence enlisted in October 1917. Following his training he was sent to the front lines in France, arriving on May 27, 1918. His father received a letter from him dated September 12 in which Lawrence said he was on the firing line but was in good health. The next correspondence Mr. Reed received was from the military on November 4, stating that Lawrence had died on October 4th.

Rosamond, the son of Mr. and Mrs. V.L. Reed of 2605 Commercial, was born in Humboldt and moved to Mattoon with his parents at the age of 16. He worked for the New York Central Railroad until he enlisted in the army. He arrived in France on May 27, 1918. Rosamond was killed in action September 29, 1918, and his parents received news of his death on November 7.

Elmer E. Hamilton
1895-1918
Co. K 125 Inft. 32 Div.

   Elmer Hamilton was killed in action in France during WWI. His wife, the former Sara Page, received a letter from the Adjutant General's office on November 26, 1918, stating that he had been officially listed as Missing in Action. The couple had been married in June just before Elmer was deployed, and a short time later Mrs. Hamilton learned she was pregnant. On March 10, 1919, Mrs. Hamilton gave birth to their daughter Katherine Juanita. During the four months since she had learned her husband was missing, Sara had received no additional information. On the line for "Father's residence address" on the birth certificate, the attending physician wrote "Reported missing in France".

   A notice was placed in the *Journal Gazette* September 15, 1921, by Elmer's family thanking everyone for their aid and support during his funeral. I could find no article about the funeral itself. I assume the three-year delay was due to complications from locating or retrieving the body after the war ended, but that's just a guess.

Roger Brion Epperson
Dec 10, 1951-Dec 24, 1971
Murdered on Christmas Eve

The front of this tombstone indicates the deceased was murdered on Christmas Eve, and the back has an engraving of an upside down peace sign. I had never heard of this case, but I was only nine when it happened. A search of newspaper articles and court records provides a glimpse of what happened.

The short answer is that twenty-year-old James Galbreath of Charleston was charged with murder by State's Attorney L. Stanton Dotson. Dotson alleged that Galbreath stabbed Roger Epperson to death during an argument in a trailer on Decker Springs Road in Charleston. A grand jury would later indict Galbreath, who claimed self-defense, with involuntary manslaughter.

Galbreath told police he and Epperson were alone at the trailer in the early morning hours of December 24, and Epperson threatened to kill him. He also said it was Epperson who had the knife and he (Epperson) attacked him with it. Galbreath said he grabbed Epperson's wrist and a struggle ensued. Galbreath said he kicked Epperson in the groin several times and didn't remember just when Epperson was stabbed. Epperson was stabbed a total of five times with death being caused by a severed jugular vein.

Several witnesses testified at a hearing as to what happened on the early morning hours of the 24th. Ricky Walker, who lived with Galbreath at a trailer on 18th Street in Charleston, testified that he arrived home around 1:00 am and Galbreath was there with his girlfriend Debbie Pearson. He said Roger Epperson was outside the trailer and Galbreath and Pearson were inside. He said the door glass was broken and Epperson had "blood all over him." Epperson said he would "kill all three of us," which Walker took to mean himself, Galbreath and Pearson. He said Epperson then choked him, shoved him and knocked his glasses off.

According to Walker, Epperson then got in his car and Galbreath went to the car and got inside. The two then began arguing. Galbreath and Epperson then drove off. Walker said as Galbreath exited the trailer Epperson said, "You better bring a butcher knife because you're going to need it." Walker said Galbreath had been able to calm Epperson down in the past and he thought he was trying to do so again.

23

Ms. Pearson said she and Galbreath were alone at Galbreath's trailer when Epperson arrived and began pounding on the door. He punched his hand through the front window. About that time Walker arrived home, and Pearson saw Epperson push Walker down and choke him. She said Epperson wiped blood on her, told her he loved her and said he was going to die for her that night.

At some point Galbreath and Epperson arrived at the home of Epperson's grandparents where Epperson asked them for their car. When they refused, Epperson flew into a rage and threatened his grandfather. His grandfather got a gun and Epperson left. His grandfather called police and asked them to find Epperson and place him in a hospital.

Epperson and Galbreath ended up back at Epperson's trailer. At some point Epperson's father arrived, but he left after he and his son got in an argument leaving the two alone. At around 5:30 am Galbreath went to his parents' home and told them about the fight he had just had with Epperson, and they called the police.

Officers went to Epperson's trailer and found him dead. A hunting knife with blood on it was found, and there was considerable disarray of furniture indicating a substantial struggle had occurred. A blood test on Epperson showed a blood alcohol content of .98 and no drugs. There was no alcohol or drugs present in Galbreath.

Sheriff Paul Smith testified that while he couldn't condone Epperson's actions that led up to the stabbing, he believed Galbreath could have left the scene at any time and avoided the fight. I suspect that was the reasoning of the grand jury when they voted to bring charges. On May 4, 1972, James Galbreath was sentenced to five years of probation for the offense. When Circuit Judge Ralph Pearman handed down the sentence he said, "based on this set of facts, the state would appear, at best, to have a very weak case of involuntary manslaughter." Pearman rejected a recommendation from county Probation Officer William Checkley to sentence Galbreath to a year in prison.

C.W.O. Richard F. Lilly
Serv. Co. 306th Inf. 77th Div.
Sept. 19, 1919-Jan. 2, 1945
Leyte, Philippine Isls.

Chief Warrant Officer Richard Lilly was killed in action at Leyte, Philippine Islands, on January 2, 1945, according to a telegram his mother received in Mattoon from the War Department. A little over a month after his death his mother, Elsie Lilly, received a letter from a Captain William Geissert, who served with Richard, explaining how he died. "Your son died in action from an exploding hand grenade and died immediately. He met his death at Libungao which is approximately six miles north of Valencia in the Onmoc valley. Burial was in the military cemetery at Valencia." Mr. Lilly had sailed for overseas duty in April 1944 and participated in the invasion of Guam in July before heading for Leyte with the 77th Division.

The January 6, 1942, edition of the *Journal-Gazette* mentioned that Private Richard Lilly had returned to duty at Fort Jackson, SC following a ten-day furlough visiting family in Mattoon. On July 16 of that year Lilly was back home. His mother hosted a dinner for family to celebrate his promotion to Sergeant. In November 1942 Lilly was promoted to the rank of Warrant Officer at Fort Jackson, SC following a special training course. Prior to this appointment he was a Staff Sergeant. In January 1944 Lilly was promoted to the rank of Chief Warrant Officer.

American forces landed on Leyte, the seventh largest island in the Philippines, on October 20, 1944, with General Douglas MacArthur wading ashore and famously proclaiming, "I have returned." The Allies were successful in expelling the Japanese army. The convergence of naval forces resulted in the Battle of Leyte Gulf, the largest naval battle in history.

Phillip Henry Rathe
1st LT U.S. Marine Corps
Vietnam N&M CM-PH
Feb 3, 1942-July 19, 1966

Twenty-four-year-old Marine Lieutenant Phillip Henry Rathe of Mattoon died a hero in Vietnam trying to save the life of one of the men under his command. Lt. Rathe was the commander of an infantry platoon in Company C, 1st Battalion, 3rd Marines in Vietnam where he had been stationed for thirteen months. He was a 1960 graduate of Mattoon High School and had been a Marine since his graduation from the University of Illinois.

On the evening of July 19, 1966, Lt. Rathe and six members of his platoon were navigating the Ca De River when their landing boat capsized for unknown reasons. According to Marines on the shore, Rathe had managed to get to the surface and was swimming to safety when he saw one of his Marines in trouble. Ignoring his own safety, Lt. Rathe turned around and swam to the distressed soldier. Both men went under and could not be saved. A recovery mission was launched, and two days later the bodies of Lt. Rathe, Lance Corporal Thomas Kemerer and PFC Charles McGuirk were recovered. Lt. Rathe was posthumously awarded a Bronze Star for bravery.

On an interesting side note, while researching Phillip Rathe I stumbled across an article dated June 15, 1978, about the closing of his family's business, Rathe Nursery, after 70 years of operation. Over the years the Rathes had donated many trees to the city, schools, churches, and parks. A new Dawn Redwood tree had recently been planted at Mattoon High School in Phillip's memory.

Curtis H. Betty D.V.M.
1894-1960
Prisoner of War, WWI

Dr. Curtis H. Betty was a veteran of WWI and was a prisoner of war. I wasn't able to find any information about his imprisonment, either in newspaper archives or in online database searches. Therefore, sadly, I have no information about where or for how long he was imprisoned, when or how he was captured or any other information about his military service. His obituary mentioned he was a WWI veteran but did not say anything about his status as a POW. Were it not for the engraving of his POW medal next to his tombstone, there would be little or no evidence to make modern day residents aware of his service and sacrifice as a prisoner of war.

Dr. Betty, age 65 when he died, was born in Kansas. He graduated from veterinary school at Michigan State University and was a veterinarian in Evanston before moving to Mattoon, residing at 3021 Pine, in 1928. He was a charter member of The American Legion and was a member of the Masonic Lodge and the Illinois State Veterinary Medical Association. His graveside service included a military color guard and military rites conducted by the American Legion and the VFW.

Jean K Lash-Gammill
1st LT U.S. Army World War II
Dec 4, 1920-Feb 14, 2017
Army Nurse

I've always had the utmost respect for veterans, especially those who have served in combat. I think it's particularly interesting to learn about females who have served on the front lines in war. Obviously the percentage of female soldiers in combat zones is much lower, so we tend to hear fewer stories about their service. Lieutenant Gammill's story is quite an interesting one. In fact, someone could write a book or screenplay about just her life story.

Jean enrolled in nurses training at Methodist Hospital in Peoria, IL with a career goal that didn't have anything to do with nursing. Her original intent was to pursue a career as an airline stewardess. As she recalled in a 1998 interview with Bonnie Clark of the *Journal-Gazette*, "In those days they wanted stewardesses who were nurses." With a year left in her training the Japanese bombed Pearl Harbor thrusting the United States into war. She said she and some of her classmates decided that if we were still at war when they graduated they would enlist in the Women's Army Nurse Corps. "It was, and we did." Jean reported for induction at Fort Custer, MI at the age of 23.

Lt. Gammill was sent to Fort Shanks, NY where she boarded the *U.S.S. Cristobal* headed for Oran, Algeria, as part of a 102-ship convoy. During the journey their convoy was attacked by German submarines. Her ship was not hit, but she recalled the horror of sitting silently in total darkness while the ship was rocked by depth charges. She said, "I just sat there wondering what I'd got myself into." Things weren't much better when she arrived in Algeria as they were in the middle of an air raid and blackout.

Jean was assigned to the 81st Station Hospital which she compared to a MASH unit. They were so close to the front line that many nights it was hard to sleep because they could hear the nearby gunfire. The hospital followed the troops as they advanced into Italy from south to north through Naples, Rome and Leghorn. On June 18, 1943, the hospital packed up and headed across North Africa for Tunisia, a 784-mile trip. In April 1944 they returned to Italy to the city of Naples.

During a layover in Rome she had an experience of a lifetime when she visited the Vatican and met personally with Pope Pius XII. Of the experience she said, "He asked my name and where I was from. I told him I was from the state of Illinois in the United States. He blessed me and my family and also blessed two rosaries I had bought for a friend back home and her new baby. I had the rosaries cupped in my left hand, and he placed his hand over mine, covering them while he blessed them. Although I am not Catholic it was a very moving moment."

On October 1, 1944, Gammill's unit set up in Leghorn, Italy, where she was assigned to an area that treated wounded German prisoners of war. She said she had no issues treating them because to her they were patients first and prisoners second. The prisoners were well cared for, and she hoped American prisoners were being treated as well in German POW camps.

Jean said the one thing she remembered most about her time serving in war was the friendships she made. "Living in tents you get so close, closer than sisters even. Friendships made during a war are bonds that last forever."

Lt. Jean Gammill passed away in 2017 at the age of 96. After the war she continued working as a nurse for a time then worked in Dr. Podesta's dental office for several years. She earned a bachelor's degree from Eastern Illinois University and taught Dental Hygiene Radiology at Lake Land College. She was a member of the First Baptist Church, VFW and Order of the Eastern Star. Her husband preceded her in death.

Robert W. Metcalf
Illinois
PFC 10 Inf, 5 Inf. Div. WWII
March 4, 1923-Nov 8, 1944

Private First Class Robert Metcalf was killed in action in France during WWII. In October 1944 his parents, Mr. and Mrs. Arthur Metcalf of rural Mattoon near Gays, were notified that their son was reported as missing in action as of September 21. This news came via a telegram from the War Department. PFC Metcalf enlisted after he graduated from high school and sailed for overseas duty in November 1943. He landed in England, then was transferred to Ireland and eventually sent to France. Around the same time the Metcalfs received word their son was missing, another son, Harry, left for induction at Chicago.

In December, approximately two months after receiving word their son was missing, Mr. and Mrs. Metcalf were notified that Robert had been officially declared killed in action on November 8. PFC Metcalf was born in Mattoon in 1923 and was a 1943 graduate of Mattoon High School. His body was returned to Mattoon from a cemetery in France in August 1948, and a funeral was held at the Presbyterian Church on September 22. PFC Metcalf was posthumously awarded a Purple Heart.

One of the things I find interesting in Dodge Grove cemetery is the various monuments and memorials scattered throughout. One of the more visible ones is this monument pictured above. It's an obelisk that resembles the Washington Monument. If you pull into the cemetery from 22nd Street it's straight ahead. You can't miss it. Like all of the memorials in Dodge Grove,

I had seen it many times but never knew anything about it or, for that matter, never really thought about it. So on one of my trips I decided to take a closer look.

An inscription on the monument reads, "Erected by Palestine Lodge No. 46 Knights of Pythias. In memory of deceased members. 1929." Names of members are printed on pieces of paper encased in glass on the east and west sides of the monument. The north side has a glass case with a plaque that tells the history of the lodge. It reads, "The order of Knights of Pythias was founded in the city of Washington, D.C. February 19, 1864 by Justus H. Rathbone. Palestine lodge # 46, Mattoon, Illinois was founded April 6, 1874. The will of Mrs. Doctor Morris provided funds to start this monument in memory of her deceased sons Edward and Charles Morris. This order was founded on friendship, charity and benevolence."

The Knights of Pythias, I later learned, is a fraternal organization and secret society. It was the first fraternal organization to receive a charter under an act of the United States Congress. It was founded by Justus H. Rathbone, who had been inspired by a play by the Irish poet John Banim about the legend of Damon and Pythias. This legend illustrates the ideals of loyalty, honor, and friendship that are the center of the order. Rathbone wrote the ritual for the Knights of Pythias while he was a schoolteacher at the Eagle Harbor Schoolhouse, in Eagle Harbor, Michigan. Below are two of the pictures encased in glass on the monument.

Joseph Withington
Newbury, Mass May 4, 1834
Mattoon June 18, 1920
Capt. Co. D, 41st IL Inf.

Captain Joseph Withington has two tombstones. One is a Civil War veteran stone which lists his rank and unit, and the other mentions that he was born in Massachusetts. An article in the January 28, 1915, edition of the *Journal-Gazette* provided a profile of the early pioneer and Union Captain. It described Captain Withington as "among the last of the hardy old pioneers who settled along the banks of Whitley Creek." He was born in Massachusetts and was of English descent. It appears he moved west after finishing school in New England, but the reason and year are not mentioned.

Withington, who never married, appears to have been a well-read man. He had a collection of books written in Greek, Latin, Spanish, Italian and German. He also had a Webster's Unabridged Dictionary and a large illustrated Holy Bible. His walls were adorned with portraits, engravings and other keepsakes including a steel engraving of his father, "made by Sartaine in the early 1840s and was among the last steel plates made by that eminent artist." You have to wonder whatever happened to all those belongings and how valuable they would be.

Withington enlisted in the Union Army in Mattoon on July 30, 1861, and was mustered in as a First Sergeant in Co. D 41st Reg. On August 8 he was transferred to Birds Nest, MO under the command of General U.S. Grant to assist in fortifying Paducah, KY. He fought in battle at Ft. Henry, Ft. Donnelson, Shiloh, Matamora, the Siege of Vicksburg and others. He was slightly

32

wounded at Ft. Donnelson. He received an honorable discharge September 12, 1864. He was a member of the Grand Army of the Republic (G.A.R.), Knights Templar and Elks Club. Captain Withington's funeral was held June 20, 1920 at the Presbyterian church, officiated by Rev. Marion Hull. There was an open casket viewing, then the body was transported to Saint Louis for cremation.

Private James H. Ervin
Sept. 20, 1922-Jan. 24, 1944
Killed in Action in Italy

Private James H. "Curly" Ervin, no relation to the author, was killed in combat during WWII. Private Ervin was inducted into the army in March 1943. His parents, Mr. and Mrs. James Ervin, 1313 N. 10th Street, Mattoon, received word February 22, 1944 that he had arrived safely in Italy. Sadly just four months later he was dead. He was killed June 24, 1944, near San Angelo, Italy, after crossing the Rapidio River. No other details of the circumstances surrounding his death were reported.

Private Ervin was born in Mattoon September 20, 1922, and lived most of his life here. Prior to enlisting he had been employed at Bennett Manufacturing Company in Harvey, IL. In 1948 his body was returned to Mattoon for burial. A funeral service was held October 7, 1948, at the Interdenominational Tabernacle with the Rev. C.C. Breen officiating.

Private Ervin's mother passed away February 16, 1946, nearly two years to the day after James died. He was survived by his father, two brothers and two sisters.

John W. Sparks	Aleta V. Sparks
Sgt Air Service	Nurse, Army Nurse Corps
World War I	World War I
1893-1974	January 1, 1890-February 1, 1978

John and Aleta Sparks. Husband and wife. World War I veterans. They are the only married couple I am aware of, at least based on information engraved on tombstones, in the cemetery who are both war veterans.

Aleta died at the age of 88 in Good Samaritan Nursing Center in Geneseo, IL. Her funeral was February 4, 1978, in Mattoon at Schilling's Funeral Home with the Rev. Roger Compton officiating. I was unable to find any additional information about her, to include her military service. Her obituary simply said she was an Army nurse in France during World War I.

John died at the age of 81 at Eastview Manor Nursing Home in Sullivan. He resided at 908 Lafayette at the time of his death. Like Aleta, I could find nothing regarding the specifics of his service in the war. There was, however, quite a bit of information about his life after. He was a very active citizen.

John retired in 1959 as a railway postal clerk. He was active in the community, having served as a Justice of the Peace, and having served several offices in the local American Legion post including trustee, adjutant and commander. An April 8, 1965, newspaper article told of his reelection to the office of Assistant Township Supervisor. Apparently on election night, which had been three nights earlier, an error in counting at the County Clerk's office resulted in an incorrect announcement that John's opponent, Dan Irons, had won by 10 votes. In reality it was John who had won by 10. The final verified tally was 2255 for John Sparks, 2245 for Dan Irons.

A 50th wedding announcement for the couple appeared in the paper October 16, 1972. An open house reception was held at the First Baptist Church on Saturday, October 21. They were married October 18, 1922, in Chicago. They had two sons and ten grandchildren.

Henry Heap
Born in Royton Lancashire, England September 13, 1820
Died September 3, 1897
Mary Buckly
Wife of Henry Heap
Born December 11, 1829
Died July 21, 1889
Loved, loving and at rest

When I saw this stone I wondered how and why someone from England came to America and ended up in Mattoon, IL. Did he come here with his parents as a child? If so, when and why did they immigrate? If he came here as an adult, I had the same questions. And, if he did come to America as an adult, did he bring his family? Was he single and his wife was someone he met here?

There wasn't a lot of information about Henry online, but I did find his obituary from September 7, 1897, and it answered some, but not all, of my questions. The headline for his obituary read, "An old citizen of Mattoon passes away."

Mr. Heap had died the previous Friday, and his funeral had been Sunday at the Congregational Church with Rev. R.W. Newlands officiating. The Odd Fellows lodge, of which he had been a long-time member, was in charge of the service.

Henry was born in Royton, near Oldham, Lancashire, England, in 1826. He married Mary Buckly on Easter Sunday, 1851. They had four children: John, Richard, Henry and Emma. At the time of his death only Richard and Henry were still alive. The family immigrated to the United States in 1855, four years after he and Mary were married, so he came to this country as an adult with a family. His obituary does not say why.

When they first arrived, they settled in Wheeling, West Virginia, where they lived for four years. They lived a year in Ohio, then moved to Litchfield, IL where Henry took a job with the Big Four railroad. He moved to Mattoon when the railroad shops were moved here, and he remained in Mattoon until he retired in 1879. He and his wife moved back to England for two years, hoping the move would improve Mary's poor health. Returning in 1881 he had a home built, although his obituary does not say where it was, and he remained in that home until he died. His wife died in 1889.

Mr. Heap served one term on the city council. He was also a member of the board of directors of the Mattoon National Bank for several years.

Colonel James Monroe
January 4, 1832-October 7, 1868

You can't make it out from the picture, but a brief biography of the life of James Monroe is printed on the stone that lies flat on the ground. It's pretty interesting reading, so I decided simply to record it verbatim:

"A childhood in Charleston, Illinois then a career as a young man running a general store in the village of Paradise. He was elected the mayor of the chartered city of Mattoon in April 1861. He was appointed as a commander of Company B with the 7th Infantry Regiment of Mattoon on July 15, 1861, with the rank of Captain. With the 7th his campaign included Belmont, Fort Henry. On March 21, 1862, he was promoted from Captain to Major for meritorious service at the battle of Fort Donelson. His last action with the 7th was Shiloh. And back home to Mattoon where he is elected Colonel, this time of the 123rd Illinois Infantry. Then on to lead the march on Perryville with Terrill's brigade on to raids and skirmishes against enemy strongholds throughout central Tennessee. Then off to join Colonel Hall in the battle against General John Morgan which ends at Milton, Tennessee then through Hoover's Gap where he and his men became part of those Union soldiers who earn the name the Lightning Brigade. Somewhere along his path Colonel James Monroe feels that perhaps he has done enough for his country. He is sick and he is weary. He wants to return to his family in Coles County. But it is not over. He cannot yet rest. So on to Murfreesboro now with Wilder's brigade Now mounted infantry six weeks of hard riding and six weeks of heavy fighting before going on to Tullahoma, Chickamauga and to Chattanooga and to Farmington when with modesty, gallantry and soldierly enterprise Colonel Monroe fell gloriously leading his men in the battle of Farmington alongside General Crook and Wilder's mounted brigade in the raid against General Wheeler in Tennessee. And at last finding rest."

An old article that recounted some of the exploits of the 123rd Regiment that was mustered in Mattoon mentioned several battles. It mentions that after the battle of Perryville, "Morgan was the next victim, and Morgan's men knew the taste of Mattoon lead for days." It was on May 6, 1863, that the unit was assigned to General Wilder in the famous Wilder's Brigade and was armed with Spencer rifles. Colonel Monroe's last words as he lay dying on the battlefield were, "Boys, refuse to yield."

Dr. Leroy F. Morse
Feb 5, 1839-July 7, 1917

Sally Ann Dora
Born in Kentucky Apr. 7, 1850
Married at Paris, KY Nov. 10, 1875
Died in Kansas, Jan. 1, 1931
James William Dora, M.D.

Initially I saw these graves and took interest for different reasons. Given the dates on Dr. Morse's stone I wondered if he had been a doctor during the Civil War. I took a picture, made some notes and moved on. Later I saw the stone for Dr. and Mrs. Dora. I thought it was interesting that her stone said where she was born, married and died but his didn't. So again, I took a picture, made some notes and planned to do research later. I also wondered if the two doctors had practiced together in Mattoon's early years.

As I was looking into Leroy Morse and the Doras, I learned that the two doctors were in fact intertwined, as they were two of the earliest doctors to settle in Mattoon, and they practiced medicine in town at the same time. Dr. Dora arrived first, and he was also very prominent in the formation of Mattoon as a town. Dr. Morse arrived shortly after Dr. Dora, and the two served the community for several years. I was unable to learn anything about Sally Dora.

Dr. Dora's obituary in the *Mattoon Gazette* on August 28, 1891, said in part, "The funeral for Dr. J.W. Dora last Sunday afternoon was probably the largest similar event ever witnessed in the city, and the immense audience that packed the Presbyterian church was pretty strong evidence that his life had not been lived in vain." It went on to say he was well known to nearly every citizen of the county.

Dr. Dora moved to Mattoon in 1856, a year before it was officially chartered as a town. He was born in Bracken County, KY in 1827 and attended college at Wesleyan College in Cincinnati, then graduated from the Ohio Medical College. He had trained under Dr. G.R.C. Todd, brother of Mrs. Abraham Lincoln. He practiced medicine for two years in Harrison County, KY before moving to Mattoon.

Dr. Dora was elected Mattoon's first mayor in 1857, and he established a Masonic lodge where he served as its first master. Politically he had identified as a Henry Clay Whig until 1886 when he switched allegiances to the democratic party. He married Miss S.A. McQuown on November 10, 1875. Two sons with her and two daughters from a previous marriage survived

38

him. He practiced all areas of medicine but specialized in obstetrics and had a reputation for caring equally for all his patients regardless of income or status. He was described as "A kind husband, a loving father, a good citizen, a friendly neighbor. His death leaves a void in our community which will be hard to fill."

During Dr. Dora's time as mayor the city set the town's boundaries, selected quarters for a town hall, established a jail in a railroad boxcar and discussed the formation of a volunteer fire department. A fire department was a priority because previous fires had claimed three lives. In 1859 he appointed J. Miller and W.M. Casto as the town's first policemen and constructed a permanent jail behind the business buildings on the north side of the 1700 block of Broadway Ave.

Dr. Dora suffered two tragedies during his time in Mattoon. Some Mattoon children had gone to the circus and later tried to recreate some of the things they had seen. Dora's son Jim tried to imitate a sword swallowing stunt, and he used a small pen knife as his sword. He leaned back and held the knife over his open mouth. The knife slipped out of his hand and went down his throat. A newspaper article simply said, "Poor Jim was carried to the cemetery. His father, Dr. Dora, was a long time getting over the bereavement."

In September 1878 Dr. Dora was driving his horse-drawn carriage down East Broadway from his home to Gibbs livery stable where he planned to put up his team. A storm was coming in, and the wind was picking up blowing dust in his eyes. He picked up the pace and approached several wagons that were hitched on the side of the road near Colson's grocery store. Two boys ran out into the street between two of the wagons, and Dora's wagon struck and ran over one of the boys, six-year-old Samuel Hamilton. Initially the boy seemed to be okay, saying he felt fine and wanted to go home. However, he collapsed shortly thereafter and was taken home in grave condition where he died within an hour. Coroner Becker convened a coroner's jury who determined the death to be an unavoidable accident.

There is no obituary for Sally Dora in the newspaper's archives. She outlived her husband by 40 years, and there is no information regarding when or why she moved to Kansas. For that matter she could have still been living in Mattoon and died in Kansas during a trip. We will never know.

Dr. Leroy Frederick Morse died in 1917 at the age of 78 in Cobden, IL where he had moved after retirement. Cause of death was listed as hardening of the arteries following an illness of eighteen months. His obituary said his body was returned to Mattoon to the home of Miss Mary Dole, 1308 Charleston Ave., a cousin of Mrs. Morse. The funeral was conducted at the Dole residence.

Dr. Morse was born in Canterbury, NH and came to Mattoon shortly after the Civil War. He had served as a surgeon during the war. He practiced medicine in Mattoon for twenty-five years, retiring in 1888 when he moved to Cobden. He was elected to the school board in 1876 and served until he left Mattoon. In 1888 he was elected to the building and loan board of directors.

Col. Harry H. Wallace
April 25, 1881-March 4, 1941

When I saw the grave of Colonel Harry Wallace, I thought there might be an outside chance he had been killed in WWII due to the fact he died in 1941. However, he would have been nearly 60 years old, and the United States did not enter the war until late in 1941. Therefore I thought it was a remote possibility at best but still decided to make some notes and do further research. Colonel Wallace is among a handful of people in this category who I assumed may have been a casualty of war but were not. He does have an interesting story, however, so I thought I would tell it.

Colonel Wallace's obituary appeared in the *Journal-Gazette* on March 5, 1941, several months before the attack on Pearl Harbor. He died at the veteran's hospital in Danville. IL at the age of 59 and had been a patient there since suffering a stroke three years prior. His body was taken to Schilling Funeral Home in Mattoon pending notification of his brother, Dr. W.G. Wallace, who was traveling in Florida and could not be located. Colonel Wallace had no other family.

Colonel Wallace was born in Humboldt. He attended schools in Humboldt and Mattoon before attending Hanover Medical College. He was a graduate of the U.S. Military Academy at West Point and was a veteran of WWI.

An interesting random article about Colonel Wallace appeared in the paper on November 2, 1936. He had reported to police that a bullet was fired through the window of his home, 3000 Western Ave., narrowly missing him as he sat in a chair the previous Saturday evening. He said he delayed reporting the incident while he "worked on a clue of my own." Wallace said the bullet created a hole four inches in diameter in the window leading him to believe it was fired from a Springfield rifle. Police Chief Britton Robinson, who investigated the matter, said he could not find where the bullet had lodged. He concluded, "It is my opinion the shot was fired by boys celebrating Halloween in the wrong way. Colonel Wallace said he had no known enemies, and if he had, I don't believe they would have tried to shoot him in this manner."

Steven Lee Sheldon
June 1, 1954-Oct. 7, 2008

It's hard to make out in the picture, but the image on the bottom left of Mr. Sheldon's stone is an engraving of the Saint Louis police department uniform patch. I wondered if he was from Mattoon originally and had been killed in the line of duty as a Saint Louis officer. I don't remember ever hearing anything about that.

Mr. Sheldon was, in fact, a Saint Louis police officer. He was shot while on duty on February 8, 1985. He survived the shooting, but the bullet lodged next to his spine causing permanent paralysis from the chest down. He suffered years of health complications from the injury including serious spikes in blood pressure due to the paralysis. These complications eventually caused him to lapse into a coma, and doctors feared he would suffer irreparable brain damage. His family agreed to disconnect life support and he passed away on October 7, 2008, twenty-three years after having been shot.

A nineteen-year-old man named Willie Lee Smith was arrested for the shooting and was charged with first degree assault, armed criminal action, unlawful use of a weapon, possession of a potent drug and resisting arrest. PCP was found on his possession when he was arrested. Lee admitted to the shooting but provided no motive.

Officer Sheldon was commissioned as a Saint Louis police officer on December 17, 1978. After graduating from the academy he was assigned to the 8th precinct. He received a Chief's letter of commendation in 1983 for exemplary performance of his duties. He retired with a medical disability on July 6, 1985, after 6.5 years of service.

Officer Sheldon was the grandson of Lucille Gilbert of 2508 Marion in Mattoon, but it's unclear what other connection he had to Mattoon. His funeral was held in Saint Louis at 9:00 am the Saturday following his passing with a 1:00 pm burial service at Dodge Grove. He was survived by a daughter, Stephanie, his parents Emil and Catherine, and siblings Emil and Kathryn. I did find obituaries online for Officer Sheldon's parents. His father died in 2012 and his mother, Catherine Gilbert Sheldon, died in 2010. Both had funerals in Saint Louis but are buried at Dodge Grove, so you can presume his mother at least, if not both parents, are from Mattoon originally.

Frederick John Purnell
Born 1848 Died Aug 25, 1942
1st person to carry news of Lincoln's assassination for Pony Express Line from Marysville to Seneca, Kansas

I was fascinated when I saw this tombstone. The Pony Express has become a glamorized piece of American history from the Old West. I imagined this man, with Mattoon ties, going west to ride with the Express, then being assigned to carry news of Lincoln's assassination to areas on the frontier to people who had not yet heard about it. It's almost the stuff of movie lore. I couldn't wait to learn more about Mr. Purnell and his small role in one of the most monumental events in American history. There was just one problem when I began my research. The dates don't line up.

The Pony Express was a mail service delivering messages, newspapers, and mail using relays of horse-mounted riders that operated from April 3, 1860, to October 24, 1861, between Missouri and California. Operated by Central Overland California and Pike's Peak Express Company, the Pony Express reduced the time for messages to travel between the Atlantic and

Pacific coasts to about 10 days. It also encouraged catalogues to be created, allowing people to buy goods and have them brought by horse to the customers.

Despite a heavy subsidy, the Pony Express was not a financial success and went bankrupt in eighteen months, when faster telegraph service was established. Nevertheless, it demonstrated that a unified transcontinental system of communications could be established and operated year-round. When replaced by the telegraph, the Pony Express quickly became romanticized and became part of the lore of the American West. Its reliance on the ability and endurance of individual young, hardy riders and fast horses was seen as evidence of rugged American individualism of the Frontier times.

Pretty interesting stuff. But as I said earlier, when I learned a bit of history about the Pony Express I couldn't help but wonder how a man could have been riding with the Express, spreading word of Lincoln's assassination, which occurred in 1865, when the Pony Express had been disbanded four years prior in 1861. In short, he couldn't. So why the inscription on his stone? That's something we will probably never know. I did learn Mr. Purnell had ties to Seneca, Kansas, and that the city of Seneca was, in fact, a stop on the Pony Express route. In fact the Pony Express museum is located in Seneca.

Mr. Purnell lived to be 94 years old. His obituary, which appeared on August 24, 1942, said he died at a hospital in Jacksonville, IL from a cerebral hemorrhage which he suffered the previous September. He was born in Reading, Berkshire, England, and his family moved to America when he was 10. They lived in Seneca, Kansas, for several years. He married Emily Brown in Kansas in 1877, and they moved to Mattoon in 1893. Mr. Purnell worked in the paint shop at the Big Four railroad. Following his wife's death in 1913, he lived with his daughter at 3217 Champaign Ave.

Mr. Purnell's obituary didn't say anything about a connection to the Pony Express. I did general internet searches as well as searches specific to riders who were known to have ridden with the Pony Express, and I couldn't find anything linking Mr. Purnell to that organization. Obviously, I don't know what the full story is. I do know no one was delivering news, goods, letters or anything else with the Pony Express when Lincoln was killed because the Express was long since defunct. I suspect this may have been an embellished tale he repeated to children and grandchildren, descendants who didn't have laptops with internet, who never gave the timing a second thought and believed the story. And who thought it was noteworthy enough to engrave on his tombstone.

This photograph was taken toward the south side of the cemetery and represents the graves of several Civil War veterans. I assume they were all killed in action, but there is nothing saying that. There are a total of twenty-six veterans buried here with dates of death ranging from 1863 to 1865. The markers bear the soldiers' names, dates of death and their unit to include state. The following states are represented: two from Massachusetts, five Indiana, three Connecticut, two New Hampshire, two Maine, nine Illinois, one Wisconsin and one didn't say.

Lester Plummer Icenogle
1920-2011
Thanks For Stopping By

     I just had to take a picture of this stone and include it in the book. Walking through a cemetery reading headstones, you see so many heartbreaking stories. Veterans who were killed in combat, people who were killed in tragic accidents, children who died. Then you see a stone like this and can't help but smile which, I suspect, was Mr. Icenogle's intention. I didn't know him, but if he wanted this engraved on his tombstone I suspect he was quite a character with a sense of humor.

     I had to know a little more about this man, and it wasn't hard to find information about him. He spent his entire working life as a grocer, first at Basket Grocery, 1513 Broadway Ave., then as the owner of Icenogle's grocery store, 3120 Marshall Ave. He was a lifetime member of the VFW and served in the South Pacific and occupied Japan during WWII as an Army Air Corps photographer.

     Mr. Icenogle lived to be 91 and was survived by his wife Eleanor, a son Mark and daughter Leslie Schupbach and several grandchildren and great-grandchildren. A line in his obituary reads, "Lester will be remembered for his kindness, honesty and great sense of humor." I don't doubt it a bit. I suspect you made the world around you brighter, sir. I'm sorry we never met, but it was my pleasure to stop by.

James F. Knight
Co. F 65 Regt.
1918-1945

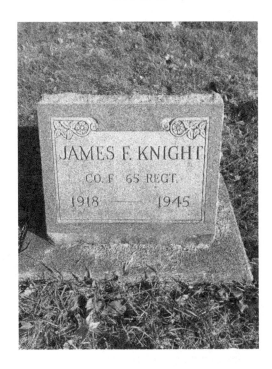

    James Knight is another example of an individual I mistakenly assumed had been killed in combat. His military unit was listed on his stone, and he died in 1945 which could have placed him in battle toward the end of the war. And he was only twenty-seven when he died. I learned that Mr. Knight had, in fact, served in WWII; however, he was killed in an accident after returning home from the war.

    Mr. Knight married Imogene Turly of Decatur on September 12, 1940. He was inducted into the army on June 22, 1944, and received an honorable discharge in January of the following year. He returned home and took a job with the Big Four railroad.

    On Tuesday, April 10, 1945, just three months after returning home from military service, Mr. Knight was injured at work. There was some confusion as to what exactly happened as no one saw the accident. Another employee found him next to the tracks severely injured. It was not clear whether he had got caught between two rail cars or stumbled and fell into the path of a train. He was rushed to Mattoon Memorial hospital where emergency surgery was performed in an attempt to save his life. A badly injured leg had to be amputated. Mr. Knight passed away a few hours later. He was survived by his wife, three-year-old son Richard and 18 month old son Robert.

46

Horace Wesley Clark
May 28, 1872-January 19, 1931

I suspect most residents, with the exception of public works employees, have never paid much attention to the cover on their water meter. If you walk out to your boulevard and look at yours, chances are it will either look like the one pictured above, saying "The Clark Meter Box", or it will be from a company called Mueller out of Decatur. If yours is one of the Clark meters, it has a tie to some interesting Mattoon history. The display pictured above sits next to the grave of Horace Wesley Clark, founder of the Clark Meter company and holder of over 50 patents. The smaller wording on the meter cover reads, "H.W. Clark Co., Mattoon, Ill Pat. Sept 3, 1891, July 11, 1905.

Mr. Clark was born in Mattoon in 1871, the third son of Judge and Mrs. Horace S. Clark. He married Inez Moore in 1891. He attended Lee's Academy in Lerna and later studied law under his father. Mr. Clark's father purchased the Mattoon waterworks plant in 1891, a business transaction that would change his son's career. It should be noted that the waterworks plant was not the water plant we think of today. It was not owned or operated by the city, and it didn't control the city's water supply. It was a manufacturing plant that produced equipment used for such purposes.

Horace W. Clark was named the superintendent of the waterworks plant when it was a small operation. He later became owner and assumed full management responsibilities. In the late 1800s water meters were located inside the home. Mr. Clark recognized the inconvenience of that, and it was his idea to install water meters outside below ground. He maintained the plant until 1912 when he sold it to the Central Illinois Public Service Company (CIPS). In 1902 he formed the H.W. Clark Company, and he registered over 50 patents for water works equipment.

In 1913 Mr. Clark built a new water plant on 12th Street, a site that would house the city's water plant for decades to come, although the original building was destroyed by the 1917 tornado. The plant helped manufacture equipment for the defense department during WWII and received a commendation from the federal government for doing so.

Horace Wesley Clark passed away on January 19, 1931, at his home, 3344 Prairie Ave. He had suffered a lengthy illness and had sought treatment at multiple hospitals including the Mayo Clinic in Minnesota. His wife survived him, as did three sons.

<h2 style="text-align:center">Carol Louise Warren</h2>
June 30, 1964-September 1, 1986

The thing that caught my eye about Ms. Warren's stone is the Lake Land College logo. I have a lot of personal history with Lake Land, being a graduate and having been an employee for twenty years. The name didn't sound familiar, so I wondered whether she had been an employee or possibly a board member. She was obviously proud of her connection with the college. I learned Ms. Warren was an incredible young lady.

Carol suffered from a disease called Ataxia. The disease confined her to a wheelchair for life and also made it impossible to write or speak clearly, although she was fully cognizant of what was going on around her. A 1981 *Journal Gazette* article talked about her one on one aid in high school, a woman named Maria Taylor, and the bond they formed. Ms. Taylor accompanied Carol to class and helped take notes for her.

When Carol was six she began to have trouble with her legs. A doctor tried using shoes with braces on them, but they didn't help and the situation got worse. Her parents finally took her to a children's hospital where the Ataxia was diagnosed. This was in the 1970s, and there was no medication that would help. In 1980 Carol suffered a stroke which left one arm paralyzed and further affected her ability to speak.

Despite the obstacles she faced, Carol continued to set goals and work hard. She ranked in the top ten percent of her high school class and had ambitions of attending college. The summer prior to her senior year she attended a camp in Bloomington that was geared toward young people in wheelchairs. While there she crossed another thing off her to-do list and went horseback riding.

After high school Carol enrolled at Lake Land College and studied Data Processing. Her mother, Virginia, attended classes with her, took notes and did keyboard work on the computer. It was Carol, however, who studied and did homework and took tests. Carol became interested in computers after a class in high school, and she aspired to work in the library at either Lake Land College or Eastern Illinois University where both libraries were digitized.

Virginia's efforts to assist Carol did not go unnoticed by the college as the Data Processing department presented her with an achievement award at their annual banquet. Virginia had no idea the award was coming and was surprised when it was presented. On Friday, May 16, 1986, Carol crossed the stage at Lake Land College in her wheelchair and received her hard earned degree.

Sadly, Carol passed away on Monday, September 1, 1986, just a few months after her college graduation. She was survived by her parents, Frank and Virginia, and a brother, James. Carol's family must have been extremely proud of her, and rightfully so. Earning a college degree is an accomplishment in the best of circumstances. Given the challenges Carol faced, it shows what guts and character she must have had. Carol was obviously so proud of her accomplishments at Lake Land that she wanted the college's logo on her tombstone.

It struck me when I learned that Carol graduated from Lake Land in 1986 because I did too. I do not have any recollection of her while I was a student there. I didn't have any computer classes so I suppose our paths never crossed. I think I would have remembered her and her mother if I would have had any classes with her, so I suspect I didn't. That's my loss. I think anyone who knew Carol or counted her among their friends would have been blessed for the experience.

Unknown Confederate Soldier

On the far east side of the cemetery lies this grave, the final resting place of an unidentified Captain in the Confederate army. In 1863 a northbound Illinois Central train was transporting approximately 1900 Confederate prisoners of war. The train stopped in Mattoon where several sick and wounded prisoners were to be taken to the Cumberland Presbyterian church at 14th and Broadway. For two years during the war the church was used as a military hospital. This soldier died on the way to the church, and his body was taken to Dodge Grove where it was buried in an unmarked grave. His identity was never known.

Fifty years later Herb Pennington, owner of Pennington Monument Yard on N. 22nd Street, erected a stone monument and placed a confederate flag next to it. Somewhere in the southern U.S. a wife, mother, son or daughter waited for news of their loved one. News that never came for a family who never knew his fate.

Robert W. Ingle
Lieutenant Air Corps
United States Army
Bomber Pilot
Feb. 13, 1916-Mar. 23, 1942

Robert Ingle graduated from Mattoon High School, then went to the University of Illinois where he earned a bachelor's degree and played on the Illinois football team. He then was accepted for flight training at the Spartan School for Aeronautics in Tulsa, OK where he completed 60 hours of flight time and 200 hours of classroom instruction. Out of 112 cadets enrolled in his class, only 65 graduated. His next post was what was known as the "West Point of the Air," at Randolph Field in Texas. Following that training he was sent to the last phase of military flight instruction at Kelly Field near San Antonio where he received his wings and was commissioned as a Second Lieutenant in the Air Corps Reserve. Lieutenant Ingle received his commission during the summer of 1941 and was one of four pilots from his graduating class to be selected to serve as flight instructors. He taught flight in Albuquerque, NM before being transferred to Midland, TX.

On a Monday in March 1942 Lieutenant Ingle was killed when the U.S. Bomber plane he was flying crashed during a training flight near Midland. Also killed in the crash were

Lieutenant William Bolton, 24, of Griffith, GA, Cadet Oliver Harja, 27, of Ironwood, MI and Cadet William Halstead, 22, of Lake City, FL.

When Lieutenant Ingle was stationed at Randolph Field he met Virginia Sitzman, the daughter of an army major who was a commanding officer there. Ingle and Sitzman were engaged to be married in June, just two months after his death. He was just three weeks shy of being promoted to First Lieutenant. He was survived by his mother Esther and father Clarence.

E.W. True
Capt. Co D 41 Ill Inf.
Civil War
1836-1862

Captain True, a Mattoon native, was killed in battle during the Civil War. In 1861 True was among the first company of Union soldiers from Mattoon to enter the war. He was commissioned a lieutenant under the command of Captain James Monroe. Before departing Mattoon for Springfield where they would receive their orders, the men met for dinner at the Pennsylvania Hotel. Lieutenant True would eventually be promoted to Captain and was killed at the battle of Fort Donelson.

Captain True's obituary appeared in the February 22, 1862, edition of the *Mattoon Gazette* and read in part, "In the midst of our great rejoicing over the victory at Fort Donelson, our community was precipitated in gloom by the melancholy tidings of the death of Captain E.W. True of Mattoon, who was killed while gallantly leading his company, at a time when the 41st was exposed to the concentrated fire of several regiments of Mississippi and Texas troops."

A letter that was later sent from the battlefield said the fatal bullet entered Captain True's left side below the ribs and lodged in his back. Apparently he lingered for several hours before succumbing to his wound. His remains were brought home by his nephew, James True. Captain True's son, Theodore, was also wounded at Fort Donelson, having taken a bullet to the jaw, but he apparently survived. The final line of his obituary reads, "in almost every city, town and village are visited the melancholy consequences of war."

James M. Sinsabaugh, June 6, 1864
Age 17 Y. 4 M.
Co. E 17 Ill. CAV.

There are many stories of young boys enlisting during the Civil War. That was obviously the case with Mr. Sinsabaugh, but I could find nothing else about him so anything beyond that is speculation. A reasonable assumption would be that he died in battle. Regardless, what is not in dispute is that he served in a military unit and died, at the age of 17, in 1864 while the war was still going.

Aug. 5, 1851-Oct. 13, 1893

Not much you can say about this one. I thought it was odd that someone went to the trouble to place a stone for this person, but they didn't bother to put a name on it. Someone knew the deceased well enough to know when he or she was born and when they died, so they surely knew their name. All we know is this person died at the age of 42. Was it a male or female? Did they have a family? Someone is buried here, and no one will ever know anything about them.

Julius Fiedler
A native of Prussia
Died March 23, 1886.
Aged 59 years, 3 months, 6 days
Rest dear husband rest

As with others in Dodge Grove, I was curious about the life story of Mr. Fiedler since he came to America from another country. When did he come? How and why did he end up in Mattoon? I couldn't find much at all about him though. No obituary in the paper. There was no mention of his wife on his headstone, and no articles mentioning anyone by the same last name in the latter half of the 1800s. A search of old archives turned up only one article with his name mentioned, and while I assume it was the same person I can't be certain.

The article appeared in the *Mattoon Gazette* October 15, 1875. It was about the local republican party celebrating recent victories in Ohio, Iowa and Nebraska. The article mentioned, "On Monday evening the little cannon and the Mattoon cornet band awakened the echoes on our streets, and the boys kindled a huge bonfire on the street in front of Doles' hall."

As Senator Steele walked to the platform to speak, Julius Fiedler, a good republican, yelled, "Give it to 'em on the Bible and the schools!" apparently in response to a recent measure to interfere with public schools, although the article didn't say what that was about. It did say that Fiedler also mentioned "the charity and forgiveness of the republican party in pardoning the hosts of rebels who deluged our country with blood and who now have the same rights and privileges as he who was most loyal and who suffered most to defend the nation."

Prussia was a prominent German state that originated in 1525 on the southeast coast of the Baltic Sea. In 1871 most German states, with the exception of Austria and Switzerland, united to create the German empire under Prussian leadership. Prussia was a global power with great influence in the 18th and 19th centuries. It was dissolved in 1932 by a decree that transferred power from the Prussian government to the German chancellor. It was formally abolished by the Allied Control Council in 1947 following WWII.

John Fiedler was a native of Prussia during its heyday as a global power. At some point in his life, no one knows when or why, he came to America. He had a wife who placed "rest dear husband rest" on his tombstone, but there is no record of who she was. We do know in 1886, at the age of 59, John Fiedler, native of Prussia, died and was buried in Mattoon.

Sgt. K. Virgil Sell
129th Inf. 33rd Div.
WWII Bougainville
Nov. 4, 1918-Apr. 6, 1944

Sergeant Virgil Sell had already served in the army seven months before the United States entered WWII following the bombing of Pearl Harbor. While the majority of veterans who are buried at Dodge Grove and who were killed in combat during WWII were killed in Europe, Sergeant Sell fought and died in the South Pacific on Bougainville Island. Bougainville was part of the Australian territory of New Guinea prior to the war, although it was geographically part of the Solomon Islands.

In March and April 1942, the Japanese landed on Bougainville as part of their advance into the South Pacific. The airfields at Kahili and on Ballale Island were bases that allowed the Japanese to conduct operations in the southern Solomon Islands and to attack the Allied lines of communication between the United States, Australia and the Southwest Pacific Area. Reduction of the main Japanese base at Rabaul was the ultimate goal of the Allied offensive in the Solomons. The Allies first launched offensives in the Solomon Islands in November 1943, and by March 1944 they had successfully captured many strategic strongholds in the Bougainville area.

On March 9, 1944, the Japanese launched a counterattack and briefly gained ground, but the Allies were successful in repelling them and recapturing the ground from them. The Japanese army, having taken heavy losses during these operations, withdrew the majority of its force into the deep interior and to the north and south ends of Bougainville. On April 5, 1944, the American 132nd Infantry Regiment successfully launched an attack to capture the Japanese-held village of Mavavia. Two days later, while continuing a sweep for enemy forces, the regiment encountered prepared enemy defenses, where they destroyed about 20 Japanese pillboxes using pole charges and bazookas. Later, the 132nd, together with elements of the Fiji Defense Force, was tasked with securing the heights west of Saua River. The Allied troops captured several hills in fierce fighting that lasted until April 18, when the last of the Japanese defenders were killed or driven off. Sergeant Sell was killed during this phase of the fighting on April 6th.

In December 2016 Sergeant Sell's sister Beverly Fleenor talked about her brother with reporter Rob Stroud of the *Journal-Gazette* for an article that was part of a remembrance of the 75th anniversary of the attack at Pearl Harbor. Prior to joining the army he worked downtown at Bidwell's candy store. He was inducted in April 1941 and was shipped out before he had time to marry his girlfriend. Two of Mrs. Fleenor's other brothers served in the military: Dale "Rug" Sell who served in the army and Gerald Sell who served in the navy.

Mrs. Fleenor, who was 14 when her brother was killed, recalled that the army sent representatives to their family farm to deliver the news of his death. She and her parents saw them pulling down the drive and knew what had happened before they even arrived at the house. Virgil was initially buried on Bougainville, but the family had his body brought home in July 1948 for burial in Mattoon. "Mom couldn't stand for him to be over there," she said.

Ralph D. Moyer
M. Sgt. US Army
World War II, Korea
Mar. 11, 1910-Mar. 14, 1992
Purple Heart, POW

Ralph Moyer was a hero in every sense of the word. He retired as a Master Sergeant following 21 years of service in the army and saw combat during two wars, first in Italy and Africa during WWII, then in Korea. During the Korean War he was captured by the Chinese and spent three years as a prisoner of war. During his imprisonment he was separated from his wife and young daughter and from a son who was born shortly after he deployed whom he had never seen.

Eleanor Moyer saw her husband in May 1950 at Camp Carson, Colorado. Little could she have imagined that it would be three years until she would see him again, and that he would soon be a POW and she would be consumed with the fear that he might never come home alive.

Following his combat service in WWII, Sergeant Moyer remained on active duty but returned home where he served as an army recruiter for a time at the recruiting office on Broadway Ave. In September 1950 he reported to Camp Carson, then was shipped to Korea with the 25th Division. Two months later a birth announcement in the local paper reported that a son was born to Mr. and Mrs. Ralph Moyer of 2701 Pine. That son would spend the first three years of his life not knowing his father except for the pictures and stories his mother would share.

A month later, December 29, 1950, Mrs. Moyer was notified by the defense department that her husband was reported as missing in action. Mrs. Moyer spent a year not knowing her husband's fate, then on December 19, 1951, she received word that he was a prisoner of war. Obviously, that wasn't an ideal piece of news, but at least he was alive and she didn't have to live with the unknown. The same day this news was delivered she also received a letter her husband had written in October as the captors had apparently allowed each prisoner to write home.

58

Sergeant Moyer mentioned that a fellow prisoner with him was Burl Lauter of Effingham. He also told his family that if he was still being held captive by Christmas he wished them a Merry Christmas and a Happy New Year.

A headline in the *Journal Gazette* on September 4, 1953, told the news Mrs. Moyer had longed to hear, "Reds return Ralph Moyer after three years." Several weeks of prisoner exchanges had been taking place, and there were only two days left when Sergeant Moyer was released. Mrs. Moyer mentioned she had been increasingly worried but never gave up hope. On Sunday, September 20, 1953, Sergeant Moyer was finally home, in his own living room, with his wife, his six-year-old daughter Madonna and three-year-old son Eddie. I don't think it's even possible to know just how he must have felt.

Sergeant Moyer was captured on November 28, 1950, when his unit was surrounded by the Chinese army. The prisoners were marched for days, deprived of adequate food and water. Soldiers suffered from malnutrition, dehydration and dysentery. After ten days about 300 men arrived at a temporary camp where they were held for 30 days. During that time 66 of the 300 American soldiers died. Sergeant Moyer was one of the Americans who were forced to bury their comrades. They were then on the move again, but only 30 soldiers, including Sergeant Moyer, were physically able to make the march. The others were left behind and Moyer later learned they too had died.

After six days of marching they arrived at their permanent camp. It was bitterly cold, 30 degrees during the day and as low as 40 below at night. The men were kept in uninsulated mud huts with no bedding. They wore the clothes they were captured in for several months. Twenty to thirty men were held in rooms that were 10x10 with no running water. The men were all infected with lice and suffered from dysentery and diarrhea. Food, when it was allowed, consisted of nothing but corn. Sick call consisted of men being allowed to see an American doctor who was also a prisoner. He had no equipment and no medication. All he could do was offer advice on how best to care for themselves. Sergeant Moyer said he recalled having to bury several more friends who died while in the prison camp. He was also tortured by his captors who tried to force him to give a false confession of having committed atrocities that never happened. He never gave in. Of the many things I read about Sergeant Moyer, the one thing that really struck me was his compassionate and forgiving attitude. He never held animosity or hatred for his captors and he appears to have been a man who didn't dwell on it. He was known as a friendly, hard-working pleasant person who was a joy to be around. His family was important to him, and he returned home from the war and from captivity with a positive attitude and a willingness to move forward instead of looking back. He got on with the rest of his life and made the most of it.

Sergeant Moyer remained on active duty after his release and retired a few years later in February 1958. He kept busy in retirement owning a sporting goods and bait shop for several years and later selling real estate. Master Sergeant Ralph Moyer died March 14, 1992, in the V.A. hospital in Danville, IL. He was 72. His first wife had passed away in 1982, and he married Hazel Bishop, who survived him, in 1984. Also surviving were his son Ed, living in Dallas, his daughter Madonna of Oklahoma City, four grandchildren and one great-grandchild.

Ralph Moyer was a bona fide American hero. I'm sure his children and grandchildren are very proud of him. I never knew him. I wish I had.

This picture appeared in the *Journal Gazette* on September 21, 1953. It was taken just after Sergeant Moyer arrived home to see his family for the first time in three years

William H. Bean
Illinois
PFC 35 Infantry Div.
World War II
Dec. 7, 1920-April 13, 1945

  Private First Class William Bean was killed in action in Germany during WWII, but I was unable to learn much information surrounding his death. The February 21, 1945, edition of the paper had a short blurb that simply said PFC Bean had arrived safely in Belgium per his wife. He would be dead less than two months later; however, I could find no obituary and no article detailing what had happened to him.

  The next article I found was dated April 12, 1949. It detailed information about his body being returned to Mattoon from Europe for burial. That article said he had been killed in action while serving with the infantry of the Ninth Army in Germany April 13, 1945, and that he had originally been buried in Holland. He was born near Mattoon, attended Mattoon schools and worked at the Brown Shoe factory after graduating from high school. Private Bean married the former Bonnie Robinson of Etna March 8, 1941. He was survived by his wife, son William Jr. and daughter Judith Ann.

Wendell F. Blakemore
PFC US Army World War II
Sep. 14, 1921-Jul. 22, 1995
Purple Heart
POW

Private First Class Wendell Blakemore served in combat during WWII. He survived the war but endured two rounds of hell in the process, the invasion of the beaches at Normandy and a German prisoner of war camp.

On June 6, 1944, the Allies stormed five beaches at Normandy, France, in a major invasion of mainland Europe. The stakes were high. And simple. Successfully get past the German defenses and establish a foothold and they had a chance of winning the war. Fail and the war was lost. Of course, the invasion was a success, but the price was extremely high. Omaha Beach was the second beach from the west among the five landing areas of the Normandy Invasion. It was assaulted on June 6, 1944, (D-Day) by units of the U.S. 29th and 1st infantry divisions. Many of those soldiers were drowned during the approach from ships offshore or were killed by defending fire from German troops placed on heights surrounding the beach. Wendell Blakemore was one of those heroic American soldiers who stormed Omaha Beach.

The largest of the D-Day assault areas, Omaha Beach stretched 6 miles between the fishing port of Port-en-Bessin on the east and the mouth of the Vire River on the west. The western third of the beach was backed by a seawall 10 feet high, and the whole beach was overlooked by cliffs 100 feet high. The Germans, under Field Marshal Erwin Rommel, had built formidable defenses to protect this enclosed battlefield. The waters and beach were heavily mined, and there were 13 strongpoints called Widerstandsnester (resistance nests). Numerous other fighting positions dotted the area, supported by an extensive trench system. The defending forces consisted of three battalions of the veteran 352nd Infantry Division. Their weapons were fixed to cover the beach with grazing fire as well as plunging fire from the cliffs. Omaha was a killing zone.

Throughout the landing, German gunners poured deadly fire into the ranks of the invading Americans. Bodies lay on the beach or floated in the water. Men sought refuge behind beach obstacles, pondering the deadly sprint across the beach to the seawall, which offered some safety at the base of the cliff. Destroyed craft and vehicles littered the water's edge and beach, and at 8:30 am all landing ceased at Omaha. The troops on the beach were left on their own and realized that the exits were not the way off. Slowly, and in small groups, they scaled the cliffs. Meanwhile, navy destroyers steamed in and, scraping their bottoms in the shallow water, blasted the German fortifications at point-blank range. By noon German fire had noticeably decreased as the defensive positions were taken from the rear. Then one by one the exits were opened.

The Americans suffered 2,400 casualties at Omaha on June 6, but by the end of the day they had landed 34,000 troops. The German 352nd Division lost 20 percent of its strength, with 1,200 casualties, but it had no reserves coming to continue the fight. There were over 10,000 Allied casualties in the entire Normandy invasion, and all five beaches were successfully captured. Six days later, on June 12, the five beachheads were connected.

I provide this brief summary to give a glimpse of the horror the brave men like Private Wendell Blakemore faced on D-Day. The courage it took to storm that beach and fight defies comprehension. Private Blakemore found himself lying in a foxhole with a leg injury, surrounded by dead colleagues. He felt a tap on his helmet and looked up to see three German soldiers standing over him. He was one of approximately 30 American soldiers who were captured, placed in a boxcar, and transported over land to a POW camp in Germany where he was held for a year. The journey to the camp took 30 days, during which the prisoners were never allowed off the train. They were fed a piece of bread every couple of days. During his year in captivity Blakemore was forced to do labor, slept in a straw bed and never once was allowed to change clothes.

One day toward the end of the war the Germans abruptly left, and the American prisoners were left behind with no food and nowhere to go. A unit of American soldiers discovered them. They didn't know there were imprisoned Americans in the area, and the prisoners didn't know anyone was coming for them. Private Blakemore received a Purple Heart for his injury as well as a Bronze Star for bravery. He commented in an interview with Carl Walworth of the *Journal Gazette* years later, "You just can't forget a lot of that stuff. And I can't watch war shows; it brings back memories."

Private Blakemore's family had received a letter from him on June 2, 1944, just four days before the Normandy invasion. His mother received word in August that he was missing in action. On May 15, 1945, she received word that he had been liberated. He had been held at Stalag VIIa at Moosburg, Germany, near Munich. His mother Edith, 604 Prairie Ave., received a short cable from her son that simply read, "Am well and safe, and hope to see you soon."

Wendell Blakemore passed away at 4:40 pm on Saturday, July 22, 1995, at the V.A. hospital in Indianapolis. Growing up in Mattoon schools, he had been a member of the high school R.O.T.C. and was a star athlete, having once won the city tennis tournament. He married Harriet Moore in 1948, and she survived him. He was also survived by two sons, Bruce and John, and a daughter, Joyce. He was a retired machine operator at Associated Spring.

Like most of the people I've learned about during this project, I never knew Mr. Blakemore, but I wish I had. I wish I could go back in time, introduce myself, shake his hand and say, "Thank you, sir, for your service and sacrifice. It is greatly appreciated."

Eugene Peterson
PFC US Army
Sep. 2, 1924-Mar. 20, 2019
Normandy Invasion
Omaha Beach

A few weeks after learning about Wendell Blakemore I was at the cemetery and saw this marker of Eugene Peterson. I wondered if the two men knew each other. Were they in the same unit? Did they storm the beach from the same watercraft? It's amazing that two men from Mattoon were at Omaha Beach on D-Day and both survived.

Eugene Peterson had never fired a gun before reporting for basic training in Georgia. It was also his first trip away from home. A short time later the nineteen-year-old would be a machine-gunner in the army infantry during the D-Day invasion. Peterson came under enemy fire before he even left the boat as it approached the beach. He jumped off the boat into water neck deep even though he couldn't swim. Carrying a full field pack, and under constant and intense enemy fire, he somehow made it ashore alive. Many of his colleagues were not so lucky as many of them were killed before they even reached the beach.

Once Private Peterson reached the beach his work had just begun. He and other soldiers started scaling a steep cliff while continuing to come under heavy fire. Peterson saw many of his buddies get shot right beside him. Once established on the mainland, Private Peterson and other soldiers regrouped and plowed ahead, eventually marching all the way to Germany where he saw Hitler's crow's nest. As though invading the beaches at Normandy weren't enough, Peterson also fought in the Battle of the Bulge.

Mr. Peterson passed away at the Odd Fellows Home at the age of 94. He and his wife Mary had been married for 67 years. Among the many medals Eugene Peterson earned for bravery were four Bronze Stars. If you're looking for a hero, you need look no further than Private Eugene Peterson.

This is another of the many interesting monuments in Dodge Grove cemetery. The Grand Army of the Republic (G.A.R.) was a fraternal organization of union veterans of the Civil War. It was founded in Springfield, IL in 1866 and grew to include hundreds of posts across the nation, predominantly in the north but with some in the south as well. It was dissolved in 1956 at the death of its last member, Albert Woolson of Duluth, Minnesota, who passed away in 1956.

Linking men through their experience of the war, the G.A.R. became among the first organized advocacy groups in American politics, supporting voting rights for black veterans, promoting patriotic education, helping to make Memorial Day a national holiday, lobbying the United States Congress to establish regular veterans' pensions, and supporting republican political candidates. Its peak membership, at 410,000, was in 1890, a high point of various Civil War commemorative and monument dedication ceremonies.

Mattoon Post 404 was established in 1884. A newspaper article dated February 22, 1884, reported that members had met the previous Friday at the K of P hall and "organized the Mattoon post of the Grand Army of the Republic, No. 404." Approximately 50 members were mustered in, and T.R. Weaver was elected commander.

A May 24, 1906, article provides information about the timing of the placement of the monument in the cemetery. It says, "The imposing monument erected by Mattoon post No. 404, G.A.R. in honor of their dead comrades is now in place in Dodge Grove adding beauty to beauty in that quiet city of the dead." The monument is a private of the Civil War in full uniform, and is life size at 5'10" tall. The cost of the monument was $500.00, and it sits on a circular terrace twenty five feet in diameter. It was formally dedicated on Memorial Day, May 30, 1906. A parade started downtown and ended at the cemetery where dedication ceremonies were held, highlighted by an address by Lieutenant Governor L.Y. Sherman.

Elder Joseph K. David

Born Sep. 15, 1869 in Rasheya, Syria. Educated in Damascus. Accepted Christ as his savior Nov. 1898 at Omaha, Neb. Buried with Christ in baptism Aug. 20, 1902 at Galva, Illinois. Ordained to the gospel ministry Sept. 18, 1902 at Galva, Illinois. Returned to Syria as a missionary of the cross under the auspices of the Baptist Missionary Convention of Illinois Apr. 14, 1904. Established two Baptist churches and opened two schools with a promising future. Returned to the U.S.A. Oct. 4, 1909. Died at Morse, Oklahoma Jan. 15, 1910. Age at death 40 years and 4 months. Though dead he yet speaketh.

With the exception of Colonel Monroe, whom you read about earlier, Elder David wins the prize for most life information engraved on a tombstone. Joseph K. David was born in Syria at the base of Mt. Hermon which straddles the borders of modern day Syria and Lebanon. Its summit is the highest point in Syria, and its southern slopes extend to the Israeli-occupied portion of the Golan Heights. Mt. Hermon is mentioned in the Bible in both the book of Chronicles and the Book of Psalms. Some believe Mt. Hermon was the Mount of Transfiguration mentioned in the Book of Matthew when Peter, James and John went up a mountain with Jesus and saw Jesus transfigured before them, during which time Moses and Elijah appeared also and spoke with Jesus.

Those who believe Mt. Hermon to be the mountain cite two reasons: it is the highest mountain in the area, and the Transfiguration took place on "a high mountain" (Matthew 17:1), and it is located near Caesarea Philippi (Matthew 16:13), where the events described in Matthew prior to the Transfiguration took place. It should be noted, however, that the Bible does not name the specific mountain so this is speculation. In fact, Mt. Tabor has also been believed by some religious scholars as far back as the third century to be the Mount of Transfiguration. Regardless, the region where Mr. David was born has been an important religious and cultural area for centuries, dating back to the time of Christ. So how did someone born in Syria in the shadows of where Jesus and his disciples walked end up buried in Mattoon?

Obituaries being what they are, his provided a glimpse of his life. Mr. David's obituary appeared in the *Journal Gazette* on Monday, January 17, 1910. He had passed away the previous Saturday. It was reported that "The Syrian brother in law of J.O. Schrock died in Oklahoma." The news came to Mrs. Schrock by a telegram from her husband, who had gone to visit Mr. David after he fell ill, who had "gone to the stricken man's bedside."

Rev. James K. David had come to America as a boy, although there is no mention why his family moved here. He attended college in Iowa where he met Ms. Schrock (her first name is not mentioned) who was originally from Mattoon. The couple lived in this area for a time as there are a handful of articles that mention him speaking to various groups. One article, in July 1903, mentioned that he was spending the summer in Trilla. It also mentioned his interesting talks of his native country and his desire to return there and serve as a missionary.

Apparently up until a few months before his death the Davids had been living in Syria, but they had recently returned because they wanted to educate their son in American schools. The family took up residence in Mattoon, and their son was enrolled in a Mattoon school. The obituary did not say how old his son was or which school he attended. Rev. David's body was returned to the Schrock home, 405 N. 20th, for the funeral with burial in Dodge Grove cemetery. Rev. David had been traveling the country speaking, raising money to continue mission work, when he became ill in Oklahoma and died.

So a boy was born in Syria in an area where Christ and His disciples walked and preached, moved to America, fell in love with a woman from Mattoon while in college in Iowa, and was buried in Dodge Grove after he died.

Robert M. Van Dorn
Locomotive Engineer
Feb. 15, 1859-July 25, 1893
Killed while in discharge of duty on the Ohio Valley Railway
Near Morganfield, Kentucky

I could find no information about the train accident that killed Mr. Van Dorn. A brief article in the local paper on July 28, 1893, three days after he died, simply said he had been killed in a wreck on the Ohio Valley line near Morganfield, KY. The article said he was married to the adopted daughter of Mr. and Mrs. James H. Clark, and that he had three children. His wife's name was not given. It also said, "Mrs. Van Dorn is left in good circumstances as the deceased had life insurance amounting to $8000 besides other property." I later found Mrs. Van Dorn's obituary. Her name was Mary, and she died in December 1930. Her obituary said the Van Dorns had moved from Mattoon to Paducah, KY, "many years ago."

Blanche Gray
Librarian for 50 years

Obviously, the library is an asset to the community, and anyone who served as librarian for half a century is an interesting and important part of the city's history. I thought it was interesting that no dates of birth or death were engraved on Ms. Gray's tombstone, only that she had been a librarian. When I conducted a search of the *Journal Gazette* archives, I found several mentions of her. Most were minor blurbs about a meeting she attended and that sort of thing.

I found an article as early as 1904 that mentioned Ms. Gray having attended a meeting of librarians in Decatur, and a 1943 article quoted her as saying many organizations and citizens had contributed 200 new books and $166 in cash to the library's Victory Book campaign. An article in October 1951 told of her recent trip to Chicago where she attended the 55th annual conference of the Illinois Library Association.

Finally I found an article, dated June 12, 1953, that gave some insight to Ms. Gray's career. The article talked about her upcoming retirement on July 1, and it noted that she had been the first librarian, having been appointed when the library opened in 1903. I later learned there had been other librarians prior to her, but they served in a temporary location in the Holmes building on the south side of the 1800 block of Broadway before the current building was built. Ms. Gray succeeded Helen Bennet as librarian when the current building opened. So while she was not the city's first librarian she was the first, and for 50 years the only, librarian in the current building.

One article said, "she has given 50 years of her life to managing and improving the local library. That is quite a record." The paper suggested that the library board should appropriate a plaque and designate the reading room as the "Blanche Gray reading room." Ms. Gray passed away May 29, 1960, at a hospital in Jacksonville, IL at the age of 81. Her obituary did not state the date of her birth, and it did not mention any survivors.

Charles L. Neeley
SPC US Army
Iraq
Dec. 29, 1984-Aug. 25, 2004
Bronze Star

On August 25, 2004, US Army Specialist Charles "Chuck" Neeley was killed in Tikrit, Iraq, when his semi tractor-trailer rolled over as he attempted to navigate a pontoon bridge. He was assigned to the Army Reserve's 454th Transportation Company. On Friday, September 3, over 300 people packed the gymnasium at Mattoon High School for Specialist Neeley's funeral. Friends and family recalled his bright and mischievous smile which usually meant he was up to something. Army chaplain Dan Harrison talked about Neeley's dedication to duty saying, "He served faithfully and honorably," and noted that at only the age of 19 he had already been promoted to the rank of Specialist. Rev. Robert Clark said, "There are a lot of people in life who never do anything; they are just here. Neeley was not one of those people. He packed a lot of living in his 19 years."

Mattoon High School Cadet Commander Sarah Grant knew Specialist Neeley as a friend and fellow ROTC member in school. She spoke of how important ROTC was to Chuck and how important he is to them. Neeley graduated from MHS in 2003 but had already begun service with the Army Reserve. He was deployed to Iraq on February 12, 2004. General William Kirkland said wearing a military uniform is never an easy task. "Those who do wear it proudly, but it has its inherent dangers."

A service with full military honors was held at the cemetery. A 21-gun salute was given, and a bugler played Taps. Specialist Neeley was awarded the Army Commendation medal and a Bronze Star. He was the first soldier from the area to be killed in the Iraq war. He was survived by his father, Charles "Shorty" Larrew, his mother Jane Neeley-Tate, six brothers and three sisters. Like so many before him in many wars over the span of time, Specialist Neeley answered the call of duty, served his country with pride and honor and made the ultimate sacrifice. For that, we all owe him a debt of gratitude.

Odd Fellows Section

A section of the cemetery on the north end was set aside for burials of people who had been members of Odd Fellows. There is an American flag and an Odd Fellows flag in the center. Several different lodge numbers are represented, so I assume members from all over the state could be buried here. The first person buried in this section was Daniel Meichal, lodge No. 94, who died November 25, 1900. His plot is located at the southeast corner of the flagpole. After him, the subsequent graves go clockwise in a circle. Once the first circle was completed, they started a second and so on. The last person who was buried here was Seth H. Lockwood who died December 28, 1945.

James L. Wells
Born Hampshire England
Died Fort Donelson
Feb. 12, 1862

There's not much information about James Wells in the newspaper archives. I found one interesting piece of information, a resolution that was published by the Masonic Lodge, but nothing else. There is no obituary and no article detailing the circumstances of his death. I also found nothing about his life in Mattoon prior to the Civil War. The resolution was published in the *Mattoon Gazette* on March 13, 1862, a month after he was killed in battle at Fort Donelson. The resolution also alludes to relatives who live in a distant land. Given that, and the fact that he was not buried with a wife or any other family, one can assume that he immigrated here alone.

The resolution reads, "Whereas it has pleased the All-Ruling power to permit our beloved brother James Wells to be called from our midst, to the battlefield in defense of our country, and there to fall a victim to the treachery of rebels in arms against this our once prosperous and happy country. Although the deceased was a native of our Mother Country, the blood of a patriot never coursed through veins, nor pulse never beat higher than did they in Bro. Wells. He was among the first to offer himself as a volunteer in the army to fight the battles of the country of his adoption, and when the term of his first service had expired, he then offered himself for the war. Such were the attachments to the country in which he lived, that he was willing to sacrifice everything, yes, even to lay down his own life, if needs be, to perpetuate this, the most prosperous and purest form of government the sun ever shown upon. Therefore,

Resolved, That in the death of Bro. Wells this country has lost a true patriot, and the fraternity a worthy and respected brother, and the community a good citizen.

Resolved, That this lodge have cause to feel deeply this loss, and that they can truly sympathize with the friends of the deceased and especially with the relatives who live in a far distant land.

Resolved, That a copy of this be furnished to the Mattoon Gazette for publication, and a copy sent to his relatives, if their address can be obtained."

So, that's about all we know about James Wells: what's engraved on his tombstone and what's contained in this resolution. At some point in his life he moved from England to America and ended up living in Mattoon. There is no record of whether he had any family, what type of work he did before the war or how old he was when he died. He was killed in battle in 1862 at Ft. Donelson, but the circumstances are unknown. His body was returned home for burial, but the local paper appears not to have printed an obituary. He was a Mason. His family in England may or may not have ever learned of his fate.

Robert L. Ely
Born Oct. 18, 1867
Engineer
Big 4 Special Express
Killed at Sanford, Ind.
Apr. 22, 1910

News accounts of train wrecks today aren't all that uncommon, and it was apparently no different over a century ago. Mr. Ely is one of a handful of railroad employees who died in accidents in the late 1800s and early 1900s. In addition to the ones I know about because something was engraved on their tombstone, I'm sure there are others who had a simple stone with name and dates of birth and death only so a century later no one knows.

Robert Ely was the engineer of a freight train that was traveling from Saint Louis to Indianapolis. His engine, train number 46, was hauling six empty express cars. Near the town of Sanford, Indiana, an open switch caused Mr. Ely's train to veer onto a sidetrack and slam into a railcar that was parked. The estimated speed at impact was 60 mph. Nine railroad construction workers were in the car that was hit. A newspaper article in the Seymour, IN *Tribune* said the car that was hit "was smashed into kindling wood." The locomotive turned over, and the other cars left the track.

Of those on Ely's train, the following list of dead and injured was reported: Robert Ely, engineer and H. Driscoll instantly killed. James B. Donnelly died at the hospital. Dallas Springate was reported as "fractured skull; will die." Samuel Moffit, Charles Jones, Harry Clark and Harry Gullet had injuries ranging from a crushed foot to burns, cracked vertebrae and broken limbs. It was reported that all of them were from Mattoon. Of the nine men on the car that was hit one died instantly, one survived the initial impact but died at the scene, and one died later at the hospital.

Another article, in the *Indianapolis News*, mentioned another member of Ely's crew, a fireman by the last name of Venable, who was uninjured. Apparently he had been thrown clear of the train when it hit the open switch and lurched. Another freight train had passed through moments before, and the switch had not been thrown after it passed. The operator, J.B. Hunt, was brought in for questioning. He said it was not his responsibility to throw the switch, but rather it was that of a crew that was working on the track. Regardless, it appears the accident was not Mr. Ely's fault.

Doak R. White
Illinois
CPL 226 Military Police Company
World War I
Oct. 22, 1884-March 30, 1960

Doak White's tombstone interested me for a personal reason. It's common to see a person's military unit listed, especially if they served in a war, but you don't see many who were military policemen. I was an M.P. in the army so I thought I would enjoy finding out a little about this fellow M.P.

I couldn't find much information about Mr. White. There were no articles about his military service in WWI, and his obituary didn't even mention it. I did learn that he ran for mayor in 1929. He faced off against a man named John Leitzell in the republican primary and lost. Mr. Leitzell lost the general election to the Rev. S.A. Haghart who was the pastor of the Trilla Methodist church and principal of Grant Park school.

Mr. White, 75 when he passed away, was a retired railroad employee. He had lived many years in Mattoon but was living in Toledo when he died. He was born in Janesville, and he married May Allen of Mattoon in 1921. He was survived by his wife, two sons, a step-son and a step-daughter.

Lawrence S. Riddle
1887-1918
Serg. CO. I
131 INF 33 DIV
Killed in France
Nov. 10, 1918

Sergeant Lawrence Riddle

Lawrence Riddle is a name known to most people who live in Mattoon. The Riddle American Legion post is named after him, as is Riddle Elementary School and the Mattoon High School yearbook. But who was this man, and why does the city of Mattoon hold him in such high esteem?

Sergeant Lawrence Riddle fought in France during WWI. On November 10, 1918, he was killed in battle near Bois de Harville on what would prove to be the next to last day of the war. The following morning at 5:00 am an agreement was signed calling for an end to the fighting beginning at 11:00 am. Thus the date and time for Veteran's Day remembrances: the 11th hour of the 11th day of the 11th month.

Sergeant Riddle was killed when he discovered an enemy machine gun nest. He led four other soldiers on an attack that led to their capture, but he was killed during the charge. The French government would later award him the Croix de Guerre medal for bravery with bronze

75

palm. First Sergeant Leroy Anderson, who served with Riddle in the 131st Infantry, said he was "one of the bravest men I have ever known." Harvey and Lillie Riddle waited for news of their son's fate after the war ended, but they received word on December 5 that their son was dead.

Lawrence Riddle was known to be a likeable man who was highly thought of by everyone who knew him. He was a star athlete in high school, playing baseball and football and running track. He also sang in high school and church choirs and acted in community plays. The American Legion post in Mattoon was chartered after the end of the war, and it was named after Lawrence. Several of his friends were charter members. Mattoon High School dedicated the yearbook to him, changing the name from the Green and Gold to the Riddle, the name it bears to this day.

Sergeant Riddle's remains were returned to Mattoon in August 1921. The mayor issued a proclamation that businesses be closed during his funeral. The funeral procession included a horse-drawn caisson, and nearly 500 local veterans put on their uniforms and marched. Sergeant Riddle was posthumously awarded the Distinguished Service Cross.

Frederick A. Nelms
Born June 22, 1904
Died June 2, 1917

Twelve-year-old Frederick Nelms was one of the victims of the tornado that devastated Mattoon on May 26, 1917. When I first saw his stone, I was intrigued with his picture. It's very rare to see a person's picture on a tombstone from this era. I took a picture and moved on thinking it would be interesting to see if I could find out anything about the boy. I didn't realize until later that he had died from injuries sustained in the tornado.

If you're from Mattoon, you have no doubt heard about the tornado. Over a six-day time period in late May and early June that year there were an extremely large number of tornadoes in the central U.S., but the most damage was done on May 26. It's estimated that during the outbreak there were at least 73 tornadoes including fifteen that were either F-4 or F-5. Initially it was believed that the tornado that struck Mattoon and Charleston started in Missouri and rolled through into Indiana spanning nearly 300 miles over an eight-hour time frame. However, scientists now believe this was instead a cluster of at least four different tornadoes. Mattoon and Charleston sustained the worst damage both in terms of property damage and lives lost. In Mattoon, an area three city blocks wide and three miles long was completely destroyed leaving 103 people dead, 400 injured and 496 houses completely destroyed. Over 2500 people were left homeless. Dozens of people were killed that day, and dozens more died in subsequent days and weeks of injuries they had sustained.

There are at least 47 victims of the tornado who are known to be buried in Dodge Grove cemetery. Ironically, the tornado, which roared through the north end of town, hit Dodge Grove directly, turning over hundreds of tombstones. Sadly, many of those who died as a result of the tornado were children, and little Frederick Nelms was just one of them. When I did a search of his name in the newspaper's archives only one hit came up. It was from a section of letters children had written to Santa that appeared in the paper on December 19, 1913. He told Santa he was a nine-year-old boy who wanted a BB gun and a pair of skates. He asked Santa to bring his big brother something nice and not to forget mama and papa. He also asked for nuts, candy, oranges and bananas. The letter was signed, "Your little friend, Frederick Alvan Nelms, 916 Dewitt Ave."

Martha Smith

While doing research on Frederick Nelms, I came across a couple of articles related to Martha Smith. She too was a victim of the tornado that struck Mattoon in 1917, and her story is fascinating. At 103 years of age, Mrs. Smith was not only the oldest victim of the tornado, she was the oldest citizen of Mattoon at the time. She was also a former slave.

In an article dated May 31, 1917, five days after the tornado hit, it was reported that Mrs. Smith had died at 2:00 am at the hospital in the old folks' home. She was at home, 1800 Dewitt Ave., when the storm hit, and she sustained a skull fracture. Mrs. Smith and her only surviving son, William, age 76 of Larned, Kansas, were both slaves during the Civil War. During the war William served as a cook in the Wisconsin Regiment. According to the article a son, Horace, had died a year before, and another son, "Wiley Smith, one of Mattoon's best known colored men, died a few years ago." Mrs. Smith was also survived by several nieces, nephews, grandchildren and great grandchildren.

I wasn't able to find any information about Mrs. Smith's life before the Civil War. It would be fascinating to go back in time and talk to her. Imagine all of the things she saw during her life. She would have been born in 1814. We were still being governed by a founding father as James Madison was President. John Marshall was Chief Justice, and Henry Clay was Speaker of the House. British troops burned Washington, D.C., including the Capitol and the White House, during the War of 1812. A month later the British bombed Fort McHenry, and the American defense inspired Francis Scott Key to write "The Star Spangled Banner." She lived through the Civil War, felt the relief of being liberated from slavery, saw the dawn of a new century and the start of the first world war.

I wonder if she was born into slavery or sold into it. Was she born in America or brought here on a slave ship? When and how did she end up in Mattoon? Are any of her descendants still living here? They say death is the great equalizer. The Mattoon tornado proved that to be true. It took children and old people, white and black. It took some children and left their parents behind to grieve, and it also took parents leaving orphaned children in its wake. And it took a 103-year-old woman named Martha Smith who lived from the administration of James Madison to that of Woodrow Wilson, who was a slave, and who made a life for herself and her family after abolition in Mattoon where she died and was buried.

I did not include a picture of Mrs. Smith's tombstone because I could not find it. I was able to ascertain what section of the cemetery she is buried in, but there are no stones in that area with her name. There are a couple of old stones in the vicinity that are so old you can't read any of the wording, but they may or may not be hers.

Captain August Emil Czerwonka
R.A. Armor U.S. Army
July 15, 1936-July 13, 1968
Killed While Serving His Country In Vietnam

In September 1967, Captain August Czerwonka suffered a broken right leg during a football game at Fort Knox, KY where he was stationed. He recovered and returned to work. Sadly, the injury was nothing compared to one he would receive less than a year later in Vietnam. On May 10, 1968, the *Journal-Gazette* reported that Captain Czerwonka was visiting in Mattoon with his mother Louisa Czerwonka, 2417 Richmond, and his sister Edith Creek. Captain Czerwonka was a thirteen-year army veteran who was scheduled to leave for Vietnam in the near future. Little could his family have known that in just two months he would be dead.

On July 15, his family received a telegram notifying them that Captain Czerwonka had been killed in action near Saigon. The captain was a company commander with the Mechanized First Infantry Division, and he was also a combat veteran of the Korean War. While on patrol he was killed when an enemy mine exploded near him. He was taken to a nearby military hospital but died shortly after being admitted.

Captain Czerwonka's funeral was held Sunday, July 21, at St. John's Lutheran Church with Rev. Ronald Schmidt officiating. In addition to his mother and sister, he was survived by his wife Elizabetha (Lisa) and his children Caterina, Arlene and Dennis. The family resided in Vallejo, CA but moved to Mattoon after his death. Captain Czerwonka had met his wife, a native of Germany, while stationed there. When he deployed to Vietnam, he told her if he died he wanted to be buried at Dodge Grove near the land where his family farmed. While fulfilling that wish, Mrs. Czerwonka would later say that "Mattoon felt like home," and she stayed.

Ensign Paul W. Monson
Fighter Plane Pilot U.S. Navy
Sept 26, 1919-May 3, 1942

Paul Monson, known to friends as "Pee Wee", grew up in Mattoon and was a star athlete in high school. He was a member of the 1937 MHS football team that had been better than any in recent memory. Paul, Charley Metzelaars and George Blair made up the backfield on that team that lost only to Urbana that year. In June 1941, Paul made the paper but not for his athletic accomplishments. It seems he was arrested for speeding one night around midnight on Dewitt Ave. by Highway Patrolman Floyd Stokes. Paul appeared before Judge Morgan Phipps, pled guilty and was fined $5.

Paul Monson joined the navy and dreamed of becoming a pilot. He attended the Wentworth Military Academy in Lexington, MO, then attended flight school at Corpus Christi, TX where he earned his wings and was commissioned an ensign. Ensign Monson received his commission in April 1942 during WWII. On April 20, 1942, Ensign Monson spoke to the Mattoon Rotary club while home on leave. He talked about his experiences during training and about earning his wings. His father was in attendance during his speech, and you can only imagine how proud he was. Sadly, less than a month later, Ensign Monson was killed during a training flight at the U.S. Navy base at Norfolk, VA.

In November 1942 Ensign Monson's parents, Mr. and Mrs. H. Ray Monson, purchased a flagpole and gave it to Mattoon High School in their son's memory. A dedication ceremony was held, and participants included members of the American Legion and the MHS ROTC band. A dedicatory speech was given by J.J. Walsh, Legion Commander, and the acceptance speech was given by H.B. Black, Superintendent of Schools. The pole was placed at the southwest corner of the high school building (which at the time was the old Central Junior High building).

Fast forward a little more than six decades and, in 2006, the old Central building was being torn down. School superintendent Larry Lilly learned about the flagpole and its history, and he spoke with Joe Coleman of Coleman Salvage and Demolition. Mr. Coleman, who now owned the property, including the pole, agreed it should be returned to the school. Custodian Steve Dobbs helped find the original plaque that accompanied the flagpole. The pole and plaque were installed near the ROTC entrance at the current high school building during Memorial Day weekend in 2006.

Ensign Monson had no children when he passed away, but a second cousin, Roy Monson and his wife Emma, were present during the rededication ceremony. Their daughter Dana Monson, a 1997 MHS graduate, was a sergeant with the U.S. Army stationed in Iraq at the time. I'm sure Ensign Monson would have been proud of Dana and of her continuing a family legacy of service.

Eunice, Eddie, Teddie and Isabella Fryman
Children of E and A Fryman

How could you see these tombstones and not be struck by the sadness and tragedy of the loss of four children, one an infant and the oldest just seven, from the same family? Medicine obviously wasn't the best over a century ago, and it was common for children to die of diseases that are easily treated today. Still, to have four children die in the same family within a span of five years, three in the same year, in the early twentieth century had to be rare. I wondered if I could find any information that might shed light on this family's misfortunes. I believe I did, and what I found is suspicious and disturbing.

I did a search of the newspaper's archives for "E A Fryman" and got a hit from January 17, 1905. It was a short blurb that simply said, "Mr. and Mrs. Ernest Fryman have a sick child at their house on Cottage Ave." 1905 was prior to the birth dates on any of the tombstones of the children of E and A Fryman, but I decided to do more digging. Next I did a search for "Ernest Fryman" between 1900 and 1920.

I found an article dated April 25, 1911, that told about a Mrs. Ernest Fryman who had been forced to walk to Coles Station with a two-month-old child due to her husband's abusiveness. The article said she was "driven from home by a brutal husband, compelled to walk miles into the country carrying a small babe in her arms, leaving five children ill at home with measles to the care of the heartless father, then returning to the city to seek assistance at the hands of the police was the experience Monday of Mrs. Ernest Fryman, 3229 Broadway."

According to the article Fryman "had trouble with his wife", forcing her to leave. She knew no one in town and decided to walk to Coles Station where she thought she might get help. The article didn't explain why that was the destination she chose. Once she got there she found no one "whom she had sufficient claims to warrant her asking them for aid." It sounds as though she may have simply hoped she would find someone there she knew, but it's not clear why she thought that. She began to walk back to town and was picked up by the evening local freight and given a ride. The police initially thought they should take her home to reconcile with her husband but apparently thought better of it. Lodging was secured for "the thoroughly worn out woman" at the Essex House. In addition to the baby she was carrying, there were five other children at home who were all said to be sick with the measles. Mrs. Fryman told police her husband had not been drinking but he was "just naturally mean."

An August 8, 1916 article recounted another domestic violence issue at the home. Ernest Fryman, 3229 Broadway, was charged with disorderly conduct after his wife reported that he kicked her in the head. He pled guilty and was fined $3, but maintained his innocence. He said his wife routinely assaulted him, and that she was trying to frame him for a positive resolution to a divorce and alimony. The article noted there had been several altercations involving the police over the years. It also said Mrs. Fryman had left her husband several months before, and he had contacted the police for assistance in finding her.

There were no other people mentioned during this time frame by the last name of Fryman with initials E. or A. Based on several other articles I learned that Mr. and Mrs. Ernest Fryman (his wife's first name was Ada) were in fact the parents of the four children buried together at Dodge Grove. They appeared to have lived at the Cottage Ave. residence for some time then moved to a house on Broadway. There are mentions of several other children in addition to these four. Possibly some of their children who were born and died earlier were buried elsewhere. There are other children who lived well into the latter half of the century. Some other blurbs from the archives form a bit of a timeline:

- Tuesday, March 31, 1903: The infant child of Mr. and Mrs. Ernest Fryman is very ill.
- Tuesday, July 28, 1903: The babe of Mr. and Mrs. Ernest Fryman is sick.
- Thursday, August 4, 1904: Mr. and Mrs. Ernest Fryman of Cottage Ave. are the parents of a baby boy born Wednesday.
- Thursday, December 13, 1906: A little daughter arrived Saturday night at the home of Mr. and Mrs. Ernest Fryman of Cottage Ave.
- Friday, April 28, 1911: A funeral for three-year-old Theodore, son of Mr. and Mrs. Ernest Fryman of Broadway Ave., was held today at the residence with burial in Dodge Grove. The child passed away at three o'clock Thursday afternoon.
- Saturday, March 12, 1912: An infant daughter of Mr. and Mrs. Ernest Fryman, 3229 Broadway, born but a few days ago, died on Friday evening. Funeral services were held this afternoon with burial at Dodge Grove.
- Wednesday, April 28, 1915: Mrs. Ernest Fryman, 3200 Broadway, was removed this morning to Memorial hospital for an emergency operation.

- September 28, 1916: Mrs. Ada Fryman filed for divorce from her husband Ernest in city court. She is also seeking custody of the couple's five children: Clarence, age 14; Elmer, age 12; Edward, age 7, Harold, age 6 and Ernest Jr., age 4. The couple was married July 10, 1900, and lived together until a recent separation due to extreme cruel treatment Mrs. Fryman received from her husband. Edward, who is one of the four Fryman children buried together, died in 1916 so he obviously died within months of this divorce filing, leaving just the other four children.
- Wednesday, April 21, 1917: The nine-year-old son of Mr. and Mrs. Ernest Fryman is quite ill from spinal meningitis.

Ada married Sidney Zike, a WWI veteran, on October 23, 1919. He died in 1942. Ada died on Saturday, November 23, 1946, at the age of 58. She had apparently been healthy and active and died of a sudden massive heart attack. In 1942 Ada suffered the loss of yet another child when her son, Ernest Jr., was killed in action in WWII. He had served an earlier enlistment, was discharged, took a job with the Big Four Railroad and enlisted back into the army when WWII broke out. PFC Fryman was killed in action in Italy. His obituary said he was survived by his father who still lived in Mattoon, his mother Ada Zike, and three brothers: Clarence, Harold and Elmer.

So in summary, here's what I was able to piece together:

- Ernest and Ada Fryman were married in 1900.
- They had four children who died and were buried next to each other at Dodge Grove. One of them died in 1916, and the other three died in 1911.
- In April 1911, Mrs. Fryman walked to Coles Station with her two-month old child who would have been born in February. Another child, Isabella, was born that same month and died after four days, so the child Mrs. Fryman walked with would have had to be a twin to Isabella.
- Mrs. Fryman walked to Coles Station with her infant child on April 25, 1911. Her son Teddie died two days later.
- Four children: Clarence, Elmer, Edward and Harold were born before any of the children at Dodge Grove died (the earliest deaths being in 1911).
- Edward died in 1916, at the age of seven, the same year the Frymans divorced.

So what can you deduce? I have to say I wonder what the extent of abuse was in the Fryman home. Mr. Fryman appears to have had a temper and was physically abusive toward his wife. Could he have also been abusive to his children? It's not a stretch. People with anger management issues are impulsive. Men who abuse their wives commonly abuse children as well. I suspect in the early 1900s domestic violence was not talked about. It was thought to be a personal matter between spouses. Deaths, even those of children, were likely not investigated like they would be today. A parent would be taken at their word that a child died of an illness or accident. Could infants in the Fryman home have been shaken? Could toddlers have been hit out of anger, causing fatal injuries? Maybe so. Maybe not. No one will ever know. There were reports of measles and meningitis so it is quite possible the deaths were all of natural causes.

What we do know is that E and A Fryman lost four children, ranging in age from four days to seven years between 1911 and 1916. In 1911 alone they had a child die in February, April and September. Mrs. Fryman was abused so badly in April 1911 that she took off walking from her home with a newborn child and walked several miles seeking help and shelter. Her other children were left in the care of an abusive man, and two days later one of those children was dead. In 1915 Mrs. Fryman was admitted to the hospital for emergency surgery. There is no record of what that surgery was for.

Whatever the causes of death were, the sad reality is four children died very young. And another child grew to adulthood and died a hero in battle during the second World War.

Private James M. Sampson
Aug. 23, 1928-Feb. 23, 1947
Killed in Leghorn, Italy

I was curious about this stone because Private Sampson's death occurred two years after the end of WWII. It would not be uncommon to see a service member killed in Italy before 1945 during the war, but two years later? While obviously no less tragic, he was killed during a peace time deployment in an accidental shooting.

The private's parents, Mr. and Mrs. James Sampson of 1212 Marshall Ave., received a telegram that their son had been killed. The telegram read, "The Secretary of War has asked me to express his deep regret that your son, PFC James M. Sampson Jr., was killed February 23, 1947, when accidentally shot in the head. A letter will follow." I couldn't find any follow up stories with details from the letter so I have no idea what circumstances surrounded the shooting. After all the local deaths of service members during the recent war, you can imagine the relief Private Sampson's parents must have felt knowing their son entered the army after the war was over.

84

Private Sampson entered the army May 14, 1946, and trained at the Aberdeen Proving Grounds in Maryland. He had been home on leave in October 1946 and left for Italy a month later. He was born in Mattoon and attended Lowell and Longfellow schools. He was survived by his parents, one brother and seven sisters. A funeral with full military rites was conducted on Sunday, May 11, 1947, at the First Christian Church.

Miriam Preston Block	**William Joseph Block**
Feb. 7, 1920-Feb. 26, 2005	Mar. 10, 1918-Mar. 24, 2015
Raleigh City Council 5 terms	1st Lt. 706th Tank Battalion WWII
Manager Preston-Block Farms	Citadel-N.C. State University

Obviously, this is a couple who had ties to Mattoon and who had moved away and had successful careers elsewhere. As I looked into their lives, I learned they were both, in fact, from this area. They lived in North Carolina when they passed away, but they had family and property in the area and returned here often.

Mrs. Block was 85 when she died. She was born in Mattoon in 1920 and attended Lincoln and Longfellow schools. She graduated from Mattoon High School in 1938. She attended Eastern Illinois University and married her husband in 1941. Mrs. Block lived the last 40 years of her life in Raleigh, NC but continued to manage the family farm in Coles and Shelby counties. She returned to Mattoon often over the years.

She was active in the Democratic Women of Wake County, was a founding member of the Eleanor Roosevelt Club, Sunday School teacher, Girl Scout leader and a tutor for English as Second Language. In 1973 she was elected to the Raleigh city council, the first woman ever to hold the office. She served a total of five terms (ten years total) winning reelection each time in a landslide.

Mr. Block was born in Mattoon in 1918 and grew up on a farm west of town. He attended Columbian School and graduated from MHS in 1936. After high school he volunteered for the army and attended officer's school. He served as a tank commander in Okinawa and the Philippines during WWII from 1942 to 1946. After the war he returned to Illinois where he earned an undergraduate degree from Eastern Illinois University and a master's and PhD from the University of Illinois. In 1951 he began his career as a professor of political science at The Citadel.

In 1957 he took a similar position at North Carolina State University where he eventually became chair of the political science department. He started the Master of Public Administration program and served as chair of the faculty senate. He was also honored with the school's first outstanding teacher award. Mr. Block was an avid handball player into his 80s. He was a master gardener and enjoyed traveling to Germany and Scotland where his ancestors had lived.

The funerals for Mr. and Mrs. Block were held at the Fairmont United Methodist church in Raleigh, NC. They were survived by three daughters and three grandchildren.

Donald C. Sanders
Illinois
PFC 5 Cav (INF) 1 Cav Div (INF)
Korea PH
April 15, 1928-Oct. 28, 1951

Private First Class Donald Sanders was killed in action during the Korean War. He had already served his country during WWII, serving in the navy from 1944 to 1946. He was drafted into the army February 5, 1951, and served in combat with the infantry. His parents, Mr. and Mrs. Robert Sanders of RR2, were notified on November 26 that he had been reported missing in action. Then on December 13 his parents received a telegram that their son had been killed on October 28. A letter they received from Donald dated October 24 told them "not to worry." I couldn't find any information that gave details surrounding Private Sanders' death.

Private Sanders had attended Lowell School in Mattoon and worked at the Brown Shoe factory. He was survived by his parents, a brother and sister at home and two sisters who lived out of state. His body arrived in Mattoon on Friday, February 15, 1952, and the funeral was conducted that Sunday at Schilling Funeral Home with full military rites conducted by the American Legion and the VFW. Private Sanders was awarded the Purple Heart.

Russell L. Williams
Illinois
SGT TRP D 4 Cav 25 Inf Div
Vietnam
BSM & OLC AM & 2 OLC 2 PH
Jan 17, 1944-June 22, 1970

Twenty-six-year-old Russel Williams of 1305 N. 11th was killed in action in Vietnam. He was inducted into the army June 19, 1967, and completed a two-year tour in Vietnam during which he was wounded in combat and was awarded a Purple Heart. When his tour was complete, he reenlisted with a request to return to Vietnam. He was promoted from PFC to Specialist 4 when he reenlisted, and he was promoted to sergeant after his return to combat. Sergeant Williams was killed when the aircraft he was in was hit by enemy ground fire on June 22. Mayor Morgan Phipps urged all flags in the city to be flown at half-staff.

Funeral services for Sergeant Williams were held Wednesday July 1, 1970, at Schilling Funeral Home with full military rites. Sergeant Williams was awarded a second Purple Heart. He was survived by his parents Ova and Margaret, three brothers and three sisters.

In Memory of Thomas Garner
Feb. 3, 1925-July 11, 1945
Lost at Sea

I could find only one article about Thomas Garner and no obituary. The article appeared August 7, 1945, and said the nineteen-year-old son of Mr. and Mrs. O.E. Garner of Vandalia had been missing at sea since July 10. The article said, "Young Garner moved with his family to Vandalia about four years ago. For eight years previously the family had lived at 1401 N. Nineteenth St." Mr. Garner was in the navy, but his rank was not given.

Mr. Garner had been on board a naval plane that disappeared over the Caribbean Sea while on a routine patrol from Banana River, FL. He was a flight engineer on the plane that was last heard from at 9:10 pm over the New Providence Islands. The navy department said an exhaustive search had been conducted with no signs of the plane.

Thomas Garner was survived by his parents and four brothers. Two brothers were still at home and two were in the navy, one serving overseas and one who was a B-29 pilot stationed at Albuquerque, NM.

W.G.K. "Danny" Stenhouse
Jan. 11, 1916-Mar. 3, 1974
British 8th Army
"The Desert Rats"

So how does a native of England who fought with the British Eighth Army end up buried at Dodge Grove cemetery in Mattoon? I did some digging and found a couple of tidbits about Mr. Stenhouse but not much. However, one thing I learned was that one of his granddaughters is Andre Metzelaars of Mattoon. Andre is a friend of mine, so I called her and she was gracious enough to provide me with her grandparents' story.

On December 24, 1939, Carole Stenhouse was born at the home of her grandparents in Tilbury, Essex, England, the daughter of W.G.K. "Danny" and Mae Stenhouse. Danny's full name was William Gordon Kitchener, named after Lord Horatio Kitchener, a British military leader and statesman who served as Secretary of State for War during World War I. A few years later Danny fought in the British Eighth Army in the North African desert during WWII where they obtained the nickname "The Desert Rats". During the war Danny's family also lived through their own bombings. They lived approximately twenty miles east of London on the River Thames, and Carole could remember German bombers flying over their home enroute to raids on London. On the return trips, the Germans would drop unused bombs on civilian targets, and the Stenhouse home was hit on at least two occasions. Carole, just a small child at the time, was injured during one of those bombings.

The Eighth Army first went into action as part of Operation Crusader, the Allied operation to relieve the besieged city of Tobruk, in November 1941, when it crossed the Egyptian frontier into Libya to attack Erwin Rommel's Panzer Division. Later that month, despite achieving a number of tactical successes, Rommel was forced to concede Tobruk and was pushed back to El

Agheila by the end of 1941. In February 1942 Rommel had regrouped his forces and pushed the Eighth Army back to the Gazala line, just west of Tobruk.

At the beginning of November 1942 the Eighth Army defeated Rommel in the decisive Second Battle of El Alamein, pursuing the defeated German army across Libya and reaching the Tunisian border in February 1943, where it came under the control of 18th Army Group. The Eighth Army outflanked the German defenses in March 1943 and after further fighting alongside the British First Army, the other 18th Army Group component which had been campaigning in Tunisia since November 1942, the German forces in North Africa surrendered in May 1943. The Desert Rats were a courageous and formidable fighting force who played a huge role in the defeat of the Nazis.

Danny Stenhouse was badly injured during the war but he survived, returned home and resumed his life. In 1960 his daughter Carole, now an adult, took a trip across Europe that would culminate in a chance meeting with an American G.I. That meeting would change the course of not only Carole's life but that of her parents as well. Carole had gone to East Germany to visit a friend and was traveling back home to England when she boarded a ferry to cross the English Channel from mainland Europe.

Gary Russell, a Mattoon native, was a soldier in the US Army stationed in Germany. Mr. Russell and some friends had wanted to see London, and they took some leave to do so. The soldiers ended up at the coast where they boarded a ferry to cross the channel. You guessed it, the same ferry Ms. Stenhouse was on. The American soldier and the English traveler met, struck up a conversation and fell for each other. They kept in touch, seeing each other periodically, and made plans to marry.

When Gary's enlistment was up, he and Carole returned to Mattoon where they established a home and got married. After Carole moved to America, her parents visited from England every 2-3 years. During these trips Mr. Stenhouse fell in love with Mattoon. He liked the homes on Western Avenue, and he expressed his desire to move here permanently when he retired. His wish was to buy one of the older homes on Western and fix it up.

Sadly, Danny died suddenly of a cerebral hemorrhage at the age of 58. Knowing her husband's desire to move to America, Mrs. Stenhouse had Danny's remains returned with his daughter to Mattoon for burial so he could rest here eternally. Mrs. Stenhouse (Mae) stayed in Mattoon for approximately nine months then went back to England. When she passed away, her remains were also brought back with her daughter Carole so she could be buried next to her husband.

The graves of Carole and Mae

Danny in uniform

Potters' Field

In the late 1800s and early 1900s it was common in cemeteries across the country to have a potters' field section where the poor were buried, and Dodge Grove was no exception. Since the burial cost for the indigent was usually borne by the cemetery or the city, burial was strictly a bare bones affair. The coffin was often a wood box and it was common for there to be no tombstone. Although records were kept with the names of the dead who were buried, since there aren't many stones you can walk through this section and have no idea how many people are buried there or who they are.

I tried to find some information about this section at Dodge Grove cemetery. I didn't find anything that told specifically when it was opened for burials, although there are references to it as early as Civil War times. A monument, pictured above, was placed in potters' field in 1901. The inscription reads, "The poor ye have with you always." A May 1902 article talked about three women, Mrs. John Miller, Miss Laura Fallen and Miss Emma Falkenburg, who had recently spent a day caring for the potters' field area. For several hours they trimmed grass, cleared out weeds and planted flowers, especially around the base of the monument. The article concluded, "Many good words were spoken for the thoughtfulness of the good women who had not forgotten the poor."

A search of local newspaper archives related to potters' field reveals a number of articles that provide an interesting glimpse into how different things were in the past. I found a 1905 article that mentioned a man simply listed as E. Durham. He was from Cincinnati, was recently killed in the Illinois Central yards and was buried in potters' field. The article said, "No word has been heard of Durham's relatives, and under the circumstances it was deemed best not to delay the burial. From every indication Durham's exact home will never be known, and his relatives will never know how or where he died. It is a truly sad ending."

In 1864 a man ended up buried in potters' field after an unusual murder. It seems a local Union soldier named Charlie Shoalmax of the 17th Illinois Cavalry shot and killed a man named Ed Stevens on Broadway Ave. while home on furlough. Stevens was a copperhead, a nickname given to northern democrats who opposed the Civil War. They believed abolitionists were the cause of the war, and Lincoln and the other republicans should be thrown out of office. They sympathized with the Confederacy and wanted Lincoln to compromise with them. As you can imagine, this didn't sit well with many northerners, especially those who had fought and seen comrades killed in battle while fighting to preserve the Union.

Known and suspected copperheads were commonly forced to swear an oath of allegiance to the Union, and apparently several had been forced to do so the previous day in Mattoon. A young boy approached Shoalmax and another soldier as they were walking on Broadway, pointed out Stevens and told them he was a copperhead. The boy urged them to "fetch him up." The soldiers caught up with Stevens near Mrs. Kelly's grog-shop. The article said Shoalmax had "been drunk for a week," and had got into trouble. Shoalmax grabbed Stevens and demanded he swear the oath. Stevens refused. He went further and told Shoalmax that if he had fought in the war he would have fought alongside the Confederates. Apparently that was too much. As Stevens turned to enter the doggery, Shoalmax pulled a pistol and shot him in the back. The bullet pierced his right lung, and he died a half hour later. Shoalmax was too drunk to make a run for it, and he was arrested by his captain. He was taken to his regimental headquarters in St. Charles, IL for trial by court martial.

When local authorities went to Cumberland County where Stevens was from to notify his relatives, they learned he had been kicked out of the neighborhood for being "a very bad character with a reputation of a common thief and had been driven from the neighborhood on account of his many depredations. They rejoiced in his death." The paper described Stevens as "a worthless fellow being in such bad repute that no one would bury him." Therefore, after lying several days with no one to claim it, his body was buried in potters' field.

Another article in 1907 told of a local black woman named Susan Alston who was nearly buried in potters' field by her cruel husband, but some friends of hers demanded a better burial. It seems Mrs. Alston's husband William was known "among the colored people as cruel to his helpmate." William had amassed a sizeable estate but had been emotionally and physically abusive to his wife, starving and beating her. Despite having considerable means, William had paid the cemetery sexton $3.50 for a plot in potters' field. Mrs. Alston appears to have been highly thought of in both the white and black communities, and her funeral was attended by numerous people.

When the mourners arrived at the cemetery, the "white women who had befriended her for years remonstrated with Alston," when they saw his wife was to be buried in an unmarked grave in potters' field. When he refused to make any other arrangements, the women stopped the sexton and told him they would pay for a decent plot themselves then sue William for the cost. Upon hearing this William paid the $25 for a regular plot. Mrs. Alston's body was then placed in the receiving vault pending preparation of her new grave.

There are other interesting stories about this section of Dodge Grove cemetery. It's sad to reflect on the many forgotten stories, forgotten to time because people were buried in unmarked graves by a community that quickly forgot they had existed.

Arland D. Williams Jr.
Sept 23, 1935-Jan 13, 1982

     Arland D. Williams' death made him a national hero. And that's not just my words, but those of no less than the President of the United States. The weather in the Washington, D.C. area on January 13, 1982, was horrible to say the least. I remember it well because I was there. I was stationed at Fort Belvoir, Virginia, just across the Potomac River from D.C. I recall it was bitterly cold with a howling wind and rapidly accumulating snow and ice. I also recall hearing that a commercial jet had crashed into the 14th Street bridge which spans the Potomac connecting Washington, D.C. with Arlington, VA. We didn't have cell phones, internet or 24/7 news channels then, but I remember watching TV on the local Washington channels which had interrupted normal programming to cover the event. Little did I know at the time that a man from my hometown was among the passengers fighting for their lives in the frigid water.

     On that day Air Florida Flight 90 took off from nearby Washington National Airport, failed to gain altitude, and crashed into the 14th Street Bridge, where it hit six cars and a truck on the bridge, killing four motorists. After the crash on the bridge, the plane then continued forward and plunged into the Potomac River. Soon only the tail section, which had broken off, remained afloat. Only six of the airliner's 79 occupants (74 passengers and 5 crew members) survived the initial crash and were able to escape the sinking plane in the middle of the river. Five of those passengers would be rescued and survive. One, Arland Williams, would not. According to the other five survivors, Williams continued to help the others reach the rescue ropes being dropped by the hovering helicopter, repeatedly passing the line to others instead of using it himself. While the other five were being taken to shore by the helicopter, the tail section of the wrecked Boeing 737 shifted and sank farther into the water, dragging Williams under the water with it.

     The next day, the *Washington Post* described his heroism (Mr. Williams' identity was not yet known):

     "He was about 50 years old, one of half a dozen survivors clinging to twisted wreckage bobbing in the icy Potomac when the first helicopter arrived. To the copter's two-man Park Police crew he seemed the most alert. Life vests were dropped, then a flotation ball. The man passed

94

them to the others. On two occasions, the crew recalled last night, he handed away a lifeline from the hovering machine that could have dragged him to safety. The helicopter crew – who rescued five people, the only persons who survived from the jetliner – lifted a woman to the riverbank, then dragged three more persons across the ice to safety. Then the lifeline saved a woman who was trying to swim away from the sinking wreckage, and the helicopter pilot, Donald W. Usher, returned to the scene, but the man was gone."

An essay in *Time* by Roger Rosenblatt dated January 25, 1982, also written before the identity of Williams was known, said:

"So the man in the water had his own natural powers. He could not make ice storms, or freeze the water until it froze the blood. But he could hand life over to a stranger, and that is a power of nature too. The man in the water pitted himself against an implacable, impersonal enemy; he fought it with charity; and he held it to a standoff. He was the best we can do."

It took over a year to establish without any doubt Mr. Williams' identity and actions. On June 6, 1983, he was posthumously awarded the United States Coast Guard's Gold Lifesaving Medal in a White House Oval Office presentation to his family by President Ronald Reagan and Secretary of Transportation Elizabeth H. Dole. President Reagan called Mr. Williams a national hero.

There have been a number of things done to honor Arland Williams since his death:

The docudrama *Flight 90: Disaster on the Potomac* aired on NBC on April 1, 1984. It displayed the heroism of Williams, portrayed by Donnelly Rhodes.

The repaired 14th Street Bridge over the Potomac River at the crash site, which had been officially named the Rochambeau Bridge, was renamed the Arland D. Williams Jr. Memorial Bridge in his honor by the city government of the District of Columbia in March 1985. Senator Ernest Hollings of South Carolina, a fellow alumnus of the Citadel, initiated the action in late 1983.

The Citadel, Williams' alma mater, created the Arland D. Williams Society to recognize graduates who distinguished themselves through community service. The Citadel also established the Arland D. Williams Endowed Professorship of Heroism in his honor.

In August 2003, the new Arland D. Williams Jr. Elementary School in Mattoon was dedicated.

Pop singer Sara Hickman's song "Last Man in the Water" is a tribute to Williams.

Born and raised in Mattoon, Mr. Williams graduated from Mattoon High School in 1953 and attended The Citadel in South Carolina. After graduation he served two years in the military and then went into banking, eventually becoming a bank examiner for the Federal Reserve System in Atlanta. His parents resided at 320 Crestview in Mattoon at the time of his death, but they had a winter home in Pompano Beach, Florida. Mr. Williams was traveling to Florida to visit them when he died. A funeral was held on Friday, January 22, 1982, at the First Presbyterian Church in Mattoon. Mr. Williams was survived by his parents, a son, Arland III, and a daughter, Leslie.

I have read many comments about Mr. Williams by people who knew him. The common thread is that no one is surprised by his heroic actions that day. He was a selfless man who always put others first. It's interesting that there is nothing flashy about his tombstone. Nothing written that indicates who he was and what he did. He was a humble man of integrity. I suspect a tombstone with no accolades is exactly what he would have wanted. But it's appropriate to give him a shoutout none the less.

Michael P. Simpson
Illinois
Sgt. CO D 14 INF 25 INF DIV
Vietnam PH
Dec. 12, 1943-Sept. 20, 1968

Sergeant Michael Paul Simpson was killed in action in Vietnam. His mother, Ethel Simpson of 1305 S. 15th, received word of her son's death by telegram two days after he was killed. The telegram said that Sergeant Simpson had been killed by enemy rocket fire but gave no other details. The sergeant's father Clyde had died on January 13 of that year.

Sergeant Simpson entered the army on June 14, 1967, and arrived in Vietnam on May 20, 1968. He was born in Mattoon and was a graduate of Mattoon High School and Murray State University. He taught school in Sullivan before joining the army. A service was held at Schilling Funeral Home with full military rites. Sergeant Simpson was survived by his mother and two sisters. He was awarded a Purple Heart.

Sgt. Guy Dean Parkerson
Sept. 23, 1946-May 11, 1968

When I saw the flag on Sergeant Parkerson's tombstone, I assumed the twenty-two-year-old military man who died in 1968 must have been killed in Vietnam. I was wrong. The Air Force sergeant, a native of Cooks Mills, was killed in a climbing accident near Bruneau, Idaho. Parkerson and three friends, all stationed at Mountain Home Air Force base, were attempting to descend into the 1000 feet deep Bruneau Canyon when he was killed, according to the local sheriff.

The climbers had reached the last ledge of the canyon wall and found they could not lower Parkerson by rope the 175 feet to the canyon floor. When they tried to pull him up, they heard a thud and could get no response. Several men went into the canyon the next day and recovered his body.

Sergeant Parkerson was survived by his mother, three brothers and a sister. One of his brothers, Ronald, was a Marine stationed in Vietnam. It's a sad irony that Ronald is the one their mother probably worried about most while she was likely very relieved that Guy was stationed in the United States out of harm's way.

Terry Lee Russell
Illinois
SP5 39 Signal BN
Vietnam
May 25, 1947-Jan. 30, 1971

Terry Russell is yet another case of a mistaken assumption. He died in 1971 while the Vietnam War was still going on. His tombstone records his rank, military unit and the fact he served in Vietnam. He was twenty-three years old. Given all that data I assumed he was killed in action. Not so. Mr. Russell died in prison after having been convicted of murdering his wife three weeks after he returned home from Vietnam. You may think this was a sad case of a man who may have been suffering from PTSD and was not the same person he had been when he went to war. And that may well be the case. I have no way of knowing. I do know this is a complicated story with a history of a previous deceased wife before his time in the military.

On December 31, 1965, at the age of eighteen, Russell married Susetta Bridges who was sixteen. She died less than a year later on October 9, 1966, at the age of 17. Her obituary said she died at Barnes Hospital in Saint Louis eight hours after giving birth to a stillborn son. On September 6, 1967, he married Helen Gale in Saint Louis. Helen, born June 11, 1952, was fifteen when they were married. On the evening of Sunday, May 3, 1970, Helen, then 17, was sitting at a table in the crowded Elcy's nightclub in Sigel when Terry walked in with a twenty-gauge shotgun and shot her in the head. Helen was pronounced dead on arrival at Saint Anthony Hospital in Effingham. Several patrons in the club seized Terry and held him until deputies arrived. Terry had been home from Vietnam three weeks. Apparently the couple was estranged, and Terry was upset because his wife was at the club with another man.

In September 1970 Terry Russell pled guilty to voluntary manslaughter and was sentenced to four to twenty years in prison. He died on Saturday, January 30, 1971, at the Menard State Penitentiary in Chester, IL. An autopsy was performed, and the cause of death was ruled to be a cerebral hemorrhage.

William H. Kiser
Illinois
PFC Veterinary Corps
World War I
January 24, 1896-March 30, 1967

William H. Kiser served in the veterinary corps during WWI. Until I saw his tombstone, I had no idea there ever was such a thing. The U.S. Army veterinary corps was established in 1916 during WWI. At the beginning there were 72 veterinary officers and no enlisted men. Within eighteen months the numbers grew to over 2300 officers and 16,000 enlisted men. Obviously, things were much different back then. The cavalry still rode horses. Mules were used to pull equipment in wagons across the rough and muddy French terrain.

The number of horses and mules in use by October 1918 was over 165,000. Just as mechanics are needed on today's battlefields to keep vehicles and machinery running, veterinarians and veterinary assistants were needed over a century ago to keep animals healthy and able to perform. Over 30 percent of the horses and mules became sick or injured resulting in the loss of over 55,000 animals. The animals suffered the same threats as soldiers including gunfire and chemical attacks. Sick and injured animals that were well enough to travel were transported back to veterinary hospitals for treatment. Following recovery, they were often put back in action.

Private Kiser appears not to have pursued a career in the veterinary sciences after his war service as his obituary said he was a retired Illinois Central Railroad employee. He was survived by his wife Ermile and one sister.

Joseph R.C. Pierce
Illinois
L CPL US Marine Corps
Vietnam PH & GS
Nov. 3, 1948-May 5, 1968

Marine Lance Corporal Joseph Pierce was killed in action in Vietnam. The nineteen-year-old son of Mr. and Mrs. Robert Smith of 2604 Richmond was killed at Quang Tri, Vietnam, while engaged in combat with the enemy. I could find no articles that gave specific details. Corporal Pierce was active in ROTC in high school, and he enlisted in the Marine Corps June 1, 1966. He was scheduled to return home in September and was engaged to marry Guyla Beddle. He was survived by his parents, five brothers and a sister.

Dale R. Williams
S SGT US Army WWII
Sep. 5, 1920-Nov. 27, 2012
White House SIG DET
Washington DC

Not many area residents, military or civilian, can claim to have once worked in the White House, but Army Staff Sergeant Dale Williams could. Sergeant Williams served in the army signal corps during WWII from 1942 to 1945. During that time he worked in the White House for nine months under President Harry Truman.

After his military service Mr. Williams went to work at the Anaconda metal hose plant in Mattoon where he retired in 1981. He married Norma Tomlin in 1945, and she preceded him in death in 1994. Mr. Williams was a member of the American Legion and VFW. He was a member of the IBEW for 75 years. He was survived by four sons.

Mr. Williams enjoyed a long and successful life, living to the age of 92. And for nine months of those 92 years he had an experience not many can match.

Arthur Morrison O'Neal Jr.
Aviation Cadet U.S.N.R.
April 12, 1922-June 15, 1943

On October 7, 1942, 11 new recruits enlisted into the navy. One of them was Arthur O'Neal of 3105 Pine Ave. He enlisted into the Aviation Cadet Corps and was awaiting a call to service. His enlistment would entail going to college while also training as a pilot in the naval reserve. He was initially sent to Murray State Teacher's College in Kentucky but was transferred to the Indiana State Teacher's College in Terre Haute in May 1943. The reason for the transfer was that he took his pre-flight training at Murray State then transferred to Terre Haute for initial flight school.

Cadet O'Neal spent the day Sunday, June 13, 1943, at home visiting his parents. Two days later he would be dead. The following Tuesday O'Neal and flight instructor A.E. Pennington of Saint Louis were in a plane that went into a spin and crashed. Authorities could not determine who had been at the controls.

Arthur O'Neal was a star athlete at Mattoon High School. In 1948 the Arthur M. O'Neal memorial trophy was established to honor the outstanding senior lineman on the Mattoon football team. Center Bob Lyons was the first recipient.

Flagpole, Main Entrance

There is a flagpole just inside the main entrance to Dodge Grove cemetery. A plaque at the base of the pole reads, "In memory of John H. Wachtler by Mrs. John H. Wachtler and sons Mark D. Lockwood and Captain L.B. Lockwood. Erected May 30, 1938." The flag provides a nice visual as visitors enter the cemetery. Like so many other things in this cemetery, I had never paid any attention to the specific details of the pole before I began my research. During one visit I noticed the plaque and was curious as to what it said. And, of course, once I found out I was curious about Mr. Wachtler, who he was and how he came to be memorialized for all time on what is likely the most prominent memorial in the cemetery.

Mr. Wachtler died in 1935, three years before the flagpole was dedicated. His obituary reads like a passage out of an Old West novel. Mr. Wachtler was a retired businessman living at 1305 Edgar. He passed away on the evening of Saturday, May 25, 1935, after being bedfast for a week. Cause of death was listed as ailments associated with advanced age. The funeral was conducted at his home.

Mr. Wachtler was born July 24, 1849, in a covered wagon in Quincy, IL. His parents, natives of France, were on their way back home to Galena, IL at the time. They had been headed for California during the Gold Rush but turned around at the Platte River due to his mother's physical condition. In 1853 he came to Mattoon from Wisconsin, and he and his father operated the old City Hotel for several years. He was survived by his wife Catherine, whom he married March 8, 1911, and two stepsons, Mark and L.B. Lockwood.

The new flagpole was officially dedicated during a ceremony on Flag Day, June 14, 1938.

Edward C. Spurgeon
TSgt. U.S. Army
World War II
Sep. 11, 1920-Nov. 12, 1945

Sergeant Edward Spurgeon is another example of someone you could assume was killed in battle. He was in the army, died in 1945 at the age of 25, and his stone clearly indicates he served in WWII. Sadly, he was a war veteran who had survived his military service only to be gunned down on a street in Illinois in what was a case of mistaken identity.

Sergeant Spurgeon died at St. Mary's hospital in E. St. Louis, IL from abdominal bullet wounds he sustained as he stood outside the Club Crescent in East Saint Louis. Raymond Belcher, a 19-year-old taxi driver, confessed to police that he shot Spurgeon because he thought he had been with a man Belcher had an argument with a few days earlier. It was a case of mistaken identity as Spurgeon and Belcher had never crossed paths.

Spurgeon lived with his grandparents, Mr. and Mrs. W.F. Spurgeon, at 1021 N. 11th as a boy and attended Longfellow Junior High in Mattoon. He was a graduate of Urbana High School. He entered the army in 1941 and served three years fighting in the Pacific campaign. He was awarded a Purple Heart with oak leaf cluster for injuries sustained in action. He had been discharged three months before he was murdered.

Sergeant Spurgeon served his country honorably for three years during WWII. He was injured by enemy fire but survived only to come home and get gunned down by a thug who thought he was someone else. He was survived by his father.

103

William Elbert Davis
SF1C US Navy
World War II
March 5, 1920-Jan. 5, 1944

Shipfitter First Class William Davis was killed during WWII in an accident at the naval base on the Hawaiian island of Kailua. I could find no specific details of the accident except that he died of compound skull fractures sustained as a result of his duties. His father, L.R. Davis of 1113 Marshall Ave., received a letter from an army chaplain who described a ceremony that was held. The letter read in part, "The gravesite is lovely, high on a hill and overlooking the sea. It is planned that the cemetery be permanent. However, after the war arrangements may be made to have the remains shipped home if loved ones so desire."

Mr. Davis was born and raised in Mattoon. He graduated from MHS, where he was an officer in the ROTC, in 1939. He enlisted in the navy a few months after graduation and was serving in his fifth year. He was survived by his father and two brothers.

A section in Dodge Grove cemetery is called Baby Heaven. As the name implies, all of those buried here are children. There are children buried all throughout the cemetery, but this is the only area exclusive to them. It is sad to walk through this part of the cemetery and think about all of the parents who lost little ones. The earliest burial I found here is that of a little girl named Earlene Caraker who was born and died on September 16, 1911.

Harry Robert Hathaway
Mar. 7, 1923-Jan. 20, 1945

First Lieutenant Harry "Bob" Hathaway, a bombardier on a B-17, was killed in action over Italy during WWII. He was a 1941 graduate of Mattoon High School and worked at Sherwin-Williams and Montgomery Ward before enlisting in the navy in April 1942. Hathaway enlisted in the aviation cadet corps at Chanute Field in Rantoul and was called to active duty on October 25, 1942. He received training in Alabama, Georgia, Arizona and California before receiving his wings and a commission as a second lieutenant in January 1944.

Lieutenant Hathaway was shipped overseas arriving in Oran, Africa, on June 14. He was shipped to Naples, Italy, on July 7 and was assigned to the 15th Air Force in Foggia, Italy. He flew 47 missions before his plane was shot down over Italy on January 20, 1945. He was officially declared killed in action in June. He had flown missions over Germany, Austria, Romania, Italy, France, Sicily, Poland, Hungary, Yugoslavia and Greece. He was awarded the Air Medal with three oak leaf clusters and two Bronze Stars. Lieutenant Hathaway was survived by his mother and his wife, Norma. His body was shipped home for burial in March 1949, arriving in Mattoon from Chicago on the Illinois Central train.

Michael K. Friese
PFC US Marine Corps
Vietnam PH
Mar. 4, 1949-Jan. 12. 1968

Eighteen-year-old Marine Private First Class Michael Friese was killed in action in Vietnam. Private Friese graduated from Mattoon High School in 1967. Shortly after graduating he felt a desire to serve his country and enlisted in the Marine Corps. After completing his initial training, Private Friese was sent to Vietnam. He had been there just two weeks when he was killed by an enemy mortar attack at a command post in Long Chu. He sustained shrapnel wounds to his head and body in the attack.

While in high school, Friese was active in ROTC and played football and basketball. He was a member of St. John's Lutheran Church. Private Friese was survived by his mother Lucy of 210 Woodlawn Ave., two brothers and a sister.

Jack E. Horsley
Lt. Col. Judge Advocate Department
Promoted to full Colonel 1997, Promoted to Brig. General 2002
World War II Purple Heart
Trial Lawyer, Lecturer, Author
And
His wife Mary Jane
She brought love into his life

Jack Horsley appears to be another one of those people you could write a book about. He had quite an interesting life, and by all accounts I have read he was a class act. During his 92 years he was an attorney, authored several books, served in WWII where he earned a Purple Heart and watched troops leave the shores of England for the Normandy invasion, was promoted to brigadier general in the army reserves and even hosted a poetry program on the radio.

Mr. Horsley attended the University of Illinois where he received his undergraduate and law degrees. While an undergraduate student he was a member of the university's debate team. A 1935 article told about Horsley, John Honnold and William Burt defeating the debate team from the University of Michigan. He practiced law for over 60 years with the firm of Craig and Craig in Mattoon. During that time he established a reputation as one of the finest trial lawyers in the state. He was named in multiple editions of *Who's Who*, had articles published in legal journals and by the Illinois State Bar Association, was renowned as an expert in the field of medical malpractice defense and argued before the United States Supreme Court.

Mr. Horsley served in the Judge Advocate General's division of the army during WWII where he held the rank of Lieutenant Colonel. Initially stationed in Scotland, he was transported to his new assignment in England as a passenger on board a B-17 bomber, known as the Flying Fortress. In an interview years later he recalled his experiences in June 1944 leading up to the D-Day invasion. Weather postponed the initial departure date, heightening anxieties. Colonel Horsley was assigned to the staging area and saw the forces leave the English coast for France. He said, "I well remember when the actual invasion took off. The tremendous number of vessels, planes, troops and facilities was almost breathtaking."

Colonel Horsley was wounded during the war, and was awarded a Purple Heart, but he wouldn't actually receive the award for 60 years. While he was working in his office one day in 1943, a German mortar round struck the building causing serious injuries to Horsley. He was told by one of his commanders he would receive the medal, but obviously there were a lot of pressing things going on in England during the height of the war. In 2003 Horsley was notified by the Department of Defense that they discovered he had never received the medal he'd earned six decades earlier. On Tuesday, February 18, 2003, his engraved medal was delivered to him in Mattoon by Federal Express. Horsley's military service began in 1937 when he was commissioned as a Second Lieutenant out of the ROTC program at the University of Illinois. He left military service with the rank of Lt. Colonel and was later promoted to the honorary rank of Brigadier General.

Mr. Horsley was licensed to practice law April 19, 1939. As though a distinguished 60-year law career and service in WWII weren't enough, he even hosted and narrated a radio poetry program for 20 years. "Interludes of Poetry" was broadcast nightly on WLBH FM. I tried to ascertain exactly how many books he authored and identified at least 29. Book number 30 having to do with Jack Horsley should be one about his life. I know I'd read it.

Francis M. Stull
PFC 358 INF 90 DIV
World War II
June 25, 1923-Nov. 9, 1944

Private First Class Francis Stull was killed in action in France during WWII. He was employed at the Sawin-Jones Company Store in Mattoon when he enlisted in the army in September 1942. After his initial training he was sent overseas where he took part in the Normandy invasion. Private Stull survived Normandy and went on to fight in France in the months that followed.

In the latter half of November 1944 Private Stull's parents, Mr. and Mrs. Virgil Stull, received word he was missing in action. At the time he was serving under the command of General George Patton. Then on December 3rd they received word their son had been killed November 9 in France during the capture of Metz. Private Stull was survived by his parents, two sisters and a brother. In January 1949, nearly four years after the war ended, Private Stull's body was returned home from Europe for burial. A funeral with military rites was held at the Assembly of God church.

Carl A. Waltrip
Illinois
Sgt. 100 CML Mortar BN
World War II
Feb. 11, 1922-Nov. 19, 1944

Ten days after Private Francis Stull was killed in action in France, another Mattoon native, Sergeant Carl Waltrip, was killed in action in Italy. Carl Waltrip was employed with the Big Four railroad when he enlisted in the army in September 1942. On March 19, 1943, Sergeant Waltrip arrived in Casablanca where he began a little over a year of fighting in Africa, including at Tunis and Bizerte. In July 1944 he was transferred to Italy. He manned a 37-millimeter anti-aircraft gun and was killed during battle.

In early December Sergeant Waltrip's parents, Mr. and Mrs. Charles Waltrip, received a letter from their son's commander, Major Russell McMurray. In part the major said, "It is with regret that I inform you of the death of your son, Sergeant Carl A. Waltrip. He was killed in action in northern Italy by enemy artillery fire. His loss is keenly felt in this battalion as he was loved and respected by all".

In November 1948 Sergeant Waltrip's body was transferred from a military cemetery in Pietramala, Italy to Mattoon for permanent burial. A funeral with full military honors was held at Schilling Funeral Home on Sunday, November 21, 1948. He was survived by his parents, two brothers and three sisters.

Roger Glen Wiley
Jan. 27, 1928-Sept. 21, 2004

Initially I walked past Mr. Wiley's grave and didn't take much notice. He was married twice, I assume his first wife passed away while they were married, and he is buried with both wives. I thought that was nice but didn't think too much about it. A little later as I walked along the next row over, I happened to look back and saw something was written on the back of his tombstone. It was this inscription that really piqued my interest. It says, "Descendant of Zachary Taylor. Great great great grandfather 12th President of the U.S. Nephew of James Madison, James Buchanan, Jefferson Davis and Robert E. Lee." Wow! Here's a man buried in Mattoon who is a descendant of both a U.S. president and Confederate States president, a founding father and a Confederate general. I couldn't help wandering who this guy was and why his story isn't well known in the area.

I wasn't able to find out much about Mr. Wiley, and found literally nothing about his genealogy. An article that appeared in the *Journal-Gazette* on September 10, 1964, said he had been hired as a professor in the speech department at Eastern Illinois University. He held a bachelor's and master's degree from Louisiana State University and had been a professor at Harding College.

An article in the *Monroe News-Star* (Monroe, LA) dated April 24, 1952, talked about Mr. Wiley directing the senior play, "Night must Fall" at Neville High School in Neville, LA where had taken a teaching job shortly after graduating from LSU. That article also provided some other information. He was born in Philadelphia but moved to Baton Rouge age the age of four. He attended University High School in Baton Rouge where he became interested in drama. He had worked various jobs during college including working at a meat packing company and working for a radio station in Lake Charles, LA.

Mr. Wiley passed away at the age of 76 at Blessing Hospital in Quincy, IL. He was survived by a son and a daughter. He was a navy veteran of WWII. If Mr. Wiley ever wrote about his family lineage, or gave any talks about it, I couldn't find any newspaper articles that covered it. Would have been fascinating to hear him speak about his family heritage.

Glendon C. Gilbert
CWO2 US Army
WWII Korea
Apr. 17, 1911-Oct. 24, 1997
Purple Heart
EX POW

Army Chief Warrant Officer Glendon Gilbert is another of the many local heroes who served so bravely during WWII. He retired after a twenty-eight-year career during which he fought in two wars, participated in the Normandy invasion on D-Day and was imprisoned as a prisoner of war. He was drafted into the army in 1942 at the age of 31.

Chief Gilbert was a member of the 82nd Airborne Division and piloted gliders. On June 6, 1944, he flew a glider behind enemy lines during the Normandy invasion, transporting soldiers and equipment. Just a few feet away from where he landed he could see patches of dead grass where the Germans had placed mines that were designed to blow up landing Allied aircraft. After landing, Gilbert and other soldiers fanned out and began to explore the surrounding countryside. In a nearby town they were approached by a French woman who told them about three German soldiers who were hiding in a nearby house. Two were wounded, and they all wanted to surrender.

The soldiers wanted to enter the house and take the enemy soldiers captive, but Gilbert convinced his lieutenant to call for reinforcements. The lieutenant agreed and when more American soldiers arrived and surrounded the house, 42 German soldiers and one officer emerged. Gilbert would later say he just had an eerie feeling about the woman's story. The Germans did not resist. Perhaps they were weary and didn't want to fight anyway. And perhaps Chief Gilbert's intuition saved his life.

Three months later Chief Gilbert was flying over Holland when his glider was shot down. A bullet hit his foot, and he sustained a broken pelvis in the landing. He was captured by the Germans and was taken to a field hospital. He was then transferred to a German POW camp where he was held captive for about eight months until the war's end in May 1945. Chief Gilbert would later say he was not treated poorly while in captivity. He believes the reason was his blond hair and blue eyes, traits highly regarded by the Nazis.

After the end of WWII Gilbert remained in the army, and he later served in the Korean War from April through October 1953. In November he was discharged from active duty but continued to serve in the National Guard. Chief Gilbert was a charter member of the Mattoon VFW post and would also serve as commander. He helped establish the first location on the northeast corner of 16th and Broadway and oversaw the eventual move to the current location on South 19th. He also served the VFW as a member of the firing squad for many years. Chief Gilbert retired from the National Guard in 1970 after 28 years of faithful military service.

Chief Warrant Officer Glendon Gilbert passed away on October 24, 1997, at the age of 86. He was survived by his wife Norma. Chief Gilbert was a Purple Heart recipient.

Margaret H. Lunan
Nurse, Army Nurse Corps
World War I
June 27, 1890-Nov. 2, 1976

I couldn't find any information about Mrs. Lunan's service in WWI. Her obituary simply said she was a nurse, and there were no articles that mentioned her time in the war. I did learn some information about the Army Nurse Corps during that conflict.

The Army Nurse Corps (ANC) was established in 1901, sixteen years before the U.S. entered WWI on April 16, 1917. The Corps was small (403 nurses on active duty and 170 reserve nurses). At the same time, there were 8,000 nurses in the nursing service reserves of the American Red Cross.

From 1914 to 1916 American civilian nurses volunteered with the American Ambulance Service in Paris and as nurses at a French Army field hospital in Belgium. American nurses also sailed to France with the American Red Cross "Mercy Ship" expedition in 1915. Some of these nurses returned to France again with the Red Cross or with the ANC in 1917- 1918 when America officially entered WWI. These forces had already been actively working in France for three years and had 900-1000 patients in each hospital.

American reserve hospital units had been established across the nation in 1916, affiliating civilian hospitals with the Army. Red Cross nurses, doctors and medical corpsmen worked together at these hospitals and volunteered to work overseas in the event of war. By May 1917 the War Department called upon the American Red Cross to mobilize six of these base hospitals for immediate shipment to France to serve with the British Expeditionary Forces. Thus U.S. military and Red Cross nurses arrived in France before the American combat troops of the American Expeditionary Forces.

Six months after the U.S. entered WWI nearly 1,100 nurses were serving overseas in nine base hospitals. One year later 2,000 Regular Army and 10,186 Reserve nurses were on active duty serving at 198 stations worldwide. By the end of the war the ranks of the Army Nurse Corps would swell to 21,480 with over 10,000 having served overseas. This was an increase of 3800% from before the war.

Ultimately, U.S. nurses worked on surgical teams, hospital trains, hospital ships, and in all sorts of hospitals: field hospitals, mobile units, base hospitals, evacuation hospitals, camp hospitals and convalescent hospitals. The formula of nurses required for war time had stayed unchanged since the American Revolutionary War at one nurse for every ten hospital beds. At first, the Army estimated that 10,000 nurses would be needed, but by the end of March 1918 the surgeon general asked for 40,000.

No U.S. Army nurses died as a result of enemy action, three were wounded by shellfire and 272 died of disease (primarily tuberculosis, influenza, and pneumonia). Members of the ANC who died during their Army service were buried with military honors. The U.S. awarded the Distinguished Service Cross (the second highest gallantry medal) to three nurses and the Distinguished Service Medal (the highest decoration in noncombat) to 23 more.

Nurses treated soldiers who were missing limbs, who had lost their sight, who had been burned from chemical attacks and who suffered from disease. The working conditions were horrible, and they were exposed to many of the same threats as front line soldiers, threats like mortar fire and chemical attacks. Through it all they provided a valuable service at great risk to their own safety. And they volunteered to do it.

Margaret Lunan was one of many women who could have obtained her credentials and gone to work at a hospital or doctor's office out of harm's way. Instead she volunteered to leave the comfort of home, travel to a war in a foreign land and serve. For that sacrifice she was every bit a hero as the many brave soldiers who have fought. She also appears to have passed that sense of service on because I found an article that mentioned that her daughter, Jean Walden, served as an army nurse during WWII.

Margaret Lunan died at the age of 86 at Mattoon Manor nursing home. She was survived by her husband, Charles, one daughter and one son.

Floyd D. Dunifer
S 1/C U.S. Navy
1920-1944

Seaman Floyd Dunifer died while serving his country in the navy during WWII, but it wasn't a bullet, mortar shell or torpedo that killed him. It was cancer. On a warm August day in 1943 Seaman Dunifer was at the train depot on Broadway Ave. in Mattoon. He was a Navy Seabee and was preparing to head overseas. His wife Virginia and their seven-month-old daughter Carol were there to see him off.

A couple months later, in October, Dunifer was home for a few days before being reassigned to duty at Pearl Harbor. That would be the last time his family would see the healthy Floyd Dunifer they knew. A little over a year later, in December 1944, Virginia received a disheartening phone call. Her husband was in a military hospital in California battling acute leukemia, a cancer that attacks the blood and bone marrow. Mrs. Dunifer flew to California, and two days later, on their daughter's second birthday, Mr. Dunifer passed away.

Mr. Dunifer's funeral was held at the Assembly of God church on Wednesday, December 27, 1944.

This memorial, dedicated to all veterans, was dedicated at a ceremony on November 8, 1986. The site has 250 graves that were donated for use by veterans. The graves and the monument were made possible through a joint effort of the Dodge Grove Cemetery Board, VFW Post 4325 and the Lawrence Riddle American Legion Post 88.

Nicole Renee' Hilligoss
December 1, 1973-June 27, 1991
Daughter of Kenneth and Kathie (Strohl) Hilligoss
Sister of Kinda Marie
Honor Student, National Honor Society, Who's Who in American High Schools
Mattoon High School Pom Pom Squad, Dance Student

Even if I didn't know Nicole Hilligoss, I have no doubt I would have been moved when I saw her tombstone and would want to write about her in this book. A seventeen-year-old girl who died before her life had even begun. She was obviously a very bright person with so much potential. But I did know her, and that moved me even more to remember her here.

I had the privilege of knowing Nikki from the time she was a little girl. Her family has been good friends for many years, and I have always thought so much of her parents and sister. Nikki was a great kid when she was little. I remember her always smiling, playful, full of fun and energy. And as she grew older she blossomed into a beautiful young lady, both inside and out. And it was that inner beauty that made her so special. Nikki was a warm and sincere person with a heart of gold. She treated everyone with respect and had such a giving heart. Most adults, myself included, aren't the caliber of human being we should be. But Nikki was.

On June 27, 1991, Nikki and her mother were out for a walk on a nice summer afternoon. As they were walking on 14th street near Lawson Park, a car left the road and struck her from behind. She likely never knew what happened. Nikki died later that evening at the hospital. The driver had a history of seizures but had a valid driver's license. His license was revoked after the accident but was reinstated less than a year later.

But this isn't about him or whether he should have been allowed to drive. It's about the loss of a wonderful person who had so much to give. I don't know why God took Nikki on that summer day many years ago. I can't even begin to comprehend it. What I do know is that Nicole Renee' Hilligoss was one of the finest people I've ever known. It was a joy to know the funny, precocious little girl she was, and I was proud to see the lovely young lady she became. The world was a brighter and better place because she was in it.

Harold Dean Cunningham
T Sgt. US Army, US Air Force
World War II, Korea
Dec. 21, 1924-April 7, 1996
Purple Heart, Ex POW

On the night of July 18, 1944, Sergeant Harold Cunningham was plummeting toward earth at 130 miles per hour from a height of 26,000 feet. Sergeant Cunningham was a gunner on a B-17 bomber that had just been shot over Germany. His only chance for survival was to grab a parachute and jump from his burning plane.

116

Based in Italy, Cunningham's crew was flying its 39th mission over Germany. The mission of the twenty-eight Allied planes that night was to bomb the Memmingen Air Drome, a Nazi air base in southern Germany, but they were intercepted by over 200 Luftwaffe fighter planes. Of the twenty-eight Allied planes, fourteen were shot down. One hundred forty-three Americans died including the tail gunner on Sergeant Cunningham's plane. Cunningham and the rest of his crew were all injured by shrapnel. Cunningham was hit when he got out of his turret to put on his parachute. Shrapnel tore through his back, arm and leg.

The only way out of the plane was through a door on the right side. The right wing was on fire, and the only option was to jump through the flames. His face was severely burned in the process. Once safely out of the plane, the danger had obviously just begun. There was no guarantee of even making it to the ground alive as the Germans were known for shooting parachuting Americans. Sergeant Cunningham didn't want to deploy his chute, thereby slowing his descent, until he absolutely had to. He curled up into a ball to provide as small a target as possible, and he pulled his ripcord at about 1000 feet, not a second too soon.

Safely on the ground, Sergeant Cunningham knew his only chance to avoid being killed or captured was to run for it. The rest of his crewmembers who had jumped from the plane were captured and taken prisoner. Somehow Cunningham avoided capture. Though badly injured, he ran south hoping eventually to make it to Switzerland. Over the next ten days he traveled south on foot, narrowly avoiding capture on three different occasions.

The fifth night on the run, Cunningham saw a cow in a farmer's field. He was hungry, thirsty and in need of nutrition. He milked the cow, emptying the milk into a plastic cigarette container, and drank several containers full. Two nights later he spotted a garden at a farmhouse. He hid until dark, then ate potatoes and carrots from the garden. It was the first food he had eaten since being shot down. About a mile from the Swiss border Cunningham encountered an elderly Swiss couple. He told them he was Swiss, and they fed him. He then took off but found the path across the border was too mountainous and he turned back, running into the same couple. Apparently they had become suspicious of him and they greeted him with a gun. They detained him and turned him over to the German military.

Sergeant Cunningham was questioned, then placed in a cattle rail car for a four-day journey to Stalag-Luft 4 where he was held as a prisoner of war. His daily food ration consisted of one slice of black bread that was 60% sawdust and one cup of potatoes or barley. Temperatures in the winter reached 22 below zero, and the prisoners were allotted nine blocks of coal per day, enough to run the furnace for about two hours.

On February 6, 1945, the prisoners were forced to leave the camp at gunpoint and march because the Russians were closing in. The prisoners were forced to march for weeks in sub-zero temperatures and nearly froze to death. After 86 days they were liberated by Allied troops who had broken through during the Battle of the Bulge.

Sergeant Cunningham finally arrived home on June 15, 1945. For his eleven months as a prisoner he received approximately $3,000 in back pay. He was also awarded the POW medal, Purple Heart, Air Medal with three silver clusters, and the Air Defense Medal. After being discharged Cunningham graduated from Eastern Illinois University with a degree in Industrial Arts. He was drafted back into the military in August 1951 during the Korean War where he served for a year as a crew chief on a C-54 cargo plane. Following his service in the Korean War, Sergeant Cunningham moved back to Mattoon and took a job at Kuhne Manufacturing and later worked at Fedders in Effingham.

Mr. Cunningham died at the age of 71 at Saint Joseph Hospital in Highland, IL. He was survived by his wife Lenore, a son and a daughter.

Harold W. House
TEC 5 US Army
World War II
Oct. 9, 1924-Jan. 14, 2017
Purple Heart
Battle of the Bulge

Harold House was a corporal in the US Army who fought in the Battle of the Bulge. I couldn't find any specific information about involvement in the battle, other than the fact that he fought in that campaign. Winston Churchill called the battle, fought in the Ardennes region of Belgium, "the greatest American battle of the war." The battle lasted six weeks from December 16, 1944, to January 25, 1945, and it was Hitler's last major offensive against the western front. His failure to divide the French, British and American forces wore down the German army and paved the way for Allied victory. Fierce combat played out in harsh winter conditions with deep snow and frigid temperatures, and the Allied troops were already exhausted and battle weary when the campaign began. As the Germans drove into the Ardennes, the Allied line took on the appearance of a large bulge, giving rise to the battle's name.

The battle proved to be the costliest ever fought by the U.S. Army, which suffered over 100,000 casualties. The formerly serene, wooded region of Ardennes was hacked into chaos by fighting as the Americans dug in against the German advance at St.-Vith, Elsenborn Ridge, Houffalize and, later, Bastogne, which was defended by the 101st Airborne Division. Hitler's mid-December timing of the attack, one of the bloodiest of the war, was strategic, as freezing rain, thick fog, deep snow drifts and record-breaking low temperatures brutalized the American troops. More than 15,000 "cold injuries", trench foot, pneumonia, frostbite, were reported that winter.

Gen. Dwight D. Eisenhower, the supreme Allied commander, and Lt. Gen. George S. Patton Jr. led the American defense to restore the front. Eisenhower gave Patton the Third Army, about 230,000 soldiers, and ordered him to head to the Ardennes. In the small, pivotal Belgian town of Bastogne, the Germans surrounded thousands of Allied troops. Eisenhower, in response, sent in more units, including the famed 101st Airborne Division. When the Germans sent a message demanding the surrender of the 101st on December 22, they got a one-word response from its commander, Brig. Gen. Anthony McAuliffe: "Nuts!" The day after Christmas, units of Patton's rapidly approaching Third Army finally arrived, broke through the German lines, and rescued the troops. Claiming victory of the battle on January 25, 1945, the Allies headed for Berlin. The war ended less than five months later with Germany's May 7 surrender.

In all more than 1 million Allied troops, including some 500,000 Americans, fought in the Battle of the Bulge, with approximately 19,000 soldiers killed in action, 47,500 wounded and 23,000-plus missing. About 100,000 Germans were killed, wounded or captured. Although there had been many battles fought over the course of the war, it was the Ardennes campaign, which infamously became known as the Battle of the Bulge, that broke the back of the Nazi war machine and signaled the beginning of the end of Hitler's reign. It was one of the all-time great battles in American military history, even becoming immortalized in Hollywood with a movie staring Henry Fonda, and Harold House of Mattoon was one of the many brave soldiers who fought there.

Harold House died at the age of 92 at Sarah Bush Lincoln Health Center. His wife preceded him in death, and he was survived by two step-sons. Mr. House's obituary only mentions that he served honorably in the U.S. Army and that he was awarded a Purple Heart. He was a lifetime member of the VFW, and for many years he was the owner and operator of his family's business, House Brothers tavern.

Otis P. Renchen
Feb. 9, 1879-Jan. 15, 1941
I.C Engineer
Killed Near Effingham, Ill

There wasn't much information in the local paper about the circumstances of Mr. Renchen's accident. While he was originally from Mattoon, he was living in Indianapolis when he died. The only article I could find with any information about his death was one about his funeral. That article said Mr. Renchen was killed when the Illinois Central train on which he was serving as engineer turned over near Effingham. No other details were given. He took a job with the Illinois Central in 1899 when he was hired to work in the roundhouse in Effingham. In 1902 he was promoted to a position as a fireman and was transferred to Palestine, IL., and shortly thereafter he was promoted to engineer.

Mr. Renchen was survived by his wife and a daughter, Mrs. Joseph Reis. Less than a month after he died, on February 4, his 62-year-old brother Willis died. He had recently retired as an engineer with the Chicago and Eastern Illinois Railroad.

Albert "Hawk" Cook
1887-1952

Baseball has always been my favorite sport. I loved to play it as a kid, and I love to watch it as an adult. I know in the first half of the twentieth century there was a minor league baseball team in Mattoon. When I came across this tombstone I wondered whether Mr. Cook had been someone prominent in baseball. Had he been a commissioner in a youth league? Was he a Hall of Fame umpire? Had he ever played professionally, possibly as a minor league player here in town? Obviously, baseball was important enough to him to have a bat, ball and glove engraved on his stone.

I couldn't find anything about Mr. Cook being involved in baseball, but I did find plenty of other things about him. Things that made him quite an interesting character but not in a good way. He was well known among local law enforcement and had a string of arrests that literally spanned years. If you search his name in the *Journal-Gazette* archives, you can scroll through several articles that pop up. I debated whether to include him in this book, but ultimately decided to do so. My goal for this book is to document interesting stories about people who are buried in local cemeteries. Most of those stories have been about acts of heroism, tragedy or prominent accomplishments. While Mr. Cook's story doesn't fall into any of those categories, it is interesting none the less. So here are but a few of his footnotes in local history.

In 1922 Albert Cook and a man named Joe Spivens stole a car and fled to Kentucky. Local authorities obtained warrants for their arrest, and they were apprehended in Monroe County, Kentucky. Coles County Sheriff Aye went to Kentucky to extradite the fugitives back to stand charges.

In 1926 Cook was arrested by policemen Hendrix and Cutright on charges of possession of liquor and reckless driving. Additional charges were filed while he was in custody including larceny and car theft. When Cook was brought to court for his arraignment, he asked permission to use the phone to call someone to post his bail. While officers were apparently not paying close attention, Cook slipped out of the building and fled. He was arrested in Arcola a few weeks later and was brought back to Coles County to face charges before a grand jury.

1927 was a busy year for the career criminal. After posting bail on his charges from the previous year he again fled the area. He was arrested in June in Anderson, Indiana, on that warrant. Deputy Sheriff George Moore was sent to Indiana to extradite him back.

On June 27 Cook was arrested by Deputy Sheriff Frank Orndorff on charges of threatening to kill a man named William Sparks and for stealing a car at the Lake Paradise park. The article mentioned that on two separate occasions in the past Cook had escaped police custody by requesting to use the phone then slipping away. After his arrest at Lake Paradise he requested again to use the phone. This request was denied.

An August 10 article mentioned a minor, Naomi Cook, who was arrested in Indiana and brought back to Coles County on a charge of writing bad checks. It was proposed that she should be admitted to the school for girls at Geneva. The article listed her father as Albert Cook who was currently in jail following an indictment for auto theft.

In 1932 Albert Cook was arrested on another theft charge, and the narrative on that one reads like a slapstick bit on an old episode of *The Andy Griffith Show*. Cook and five other men were arrested at the home of a man named Thomas Beatty at 1009 Dewitt Ave on the morning of Monday, January 18. Apparently a few days prior a hen house owned by C.J. Taylor who lived a couple blocks down at 805 Dewitt was entered and some of Mr. Taylor's chickens were stolen.

Police got their big break in the case when they questioned a woman named Florence Andrews who told them she had cooked not one, but two, chicken dinners at the Beatty house. She had cooked the first chicken at 4:00 o'clock Sunday afternoon, and she was requested to return later that evening and cook another one. Based on Florence's statement the police obtained a search warrant and raided the Beatty home where they recovered two chickens and a duck which Mr. Taylor identified as being his. When questioned by police, Cook admitted he was the one who stole them. The newspaper article concluded, "All six of the men arrested Monday morning attended the chicken dinner Sunday night." Seriously folks, I didn't make any of this up.

Unfortunately, Cook's criminal behavior was anything but amusing in the years to come. In August 1934 he was arrested for assault with a gun on A.L. Colvin at the victim's home at 813 N. 10th. In December of that year he was sentenced to a year at the state penal farm in Vandalia for stealing gasoline from a storage shed at the Big Four railroad yard. He begged the judge for "another chance", but the request was denied.

In April 1936 Cook was arrested following a complaint filed by a sixteen-year-old girl. The girl claimed she was parked in a car with a male near a tavern north of the city on March 28 when a man, later identified as Cook, approached the car and identified himself as a police officer. Cook then forced her to drive him to "a lonely spot" three miles northeast of the city where he assaulted her. The newspaper article did not specifically state the assault was sexual.

In May 1937 Cook was arrested for yet another assault. Police were called to a home at 2213 Broadway where the occupant, a mother of several young children, reported Cook had entered her home. When she resisted his advances, he pulled her hair and choked her. Neighbors heard her screams and called police. When they arrived Cook had fled, but he was later spotted and arrested by Constable B.D. Cunningham. In October 1938 Cook was arrested for the assault of another woman in her home on Dewitt Avenue.

An article dated February 14, 1939, reported that Cook was sentenced to 35 years at the state prison at Menard for criminal assault. The article didn't say, but I assume this was the assault the previous October of the woman on Dewitt Avenue. I could find no obituary for Cook online. He died thirteen years after being sentenced to a 35-year term so one could assume he died in prison, but I couldn't find any information that confirms that.

Albert Cook appears to have been a man who never contributed much. He never stormed a beachhead. He never commanded a platoon in Vietnam or served on a battleship in the Pacific. He did steal things and assault people. And, apparently, he liked baseball.

Donald B. Van Laningham
Illinois
PFC QM Corps
World War II
June 13, 1915-June 9, 1944

Private First Class Donald Van Laningham served at Normandy during the D-Day invasion. He was a member of an Airborne Quartermaster unit and had landed ahead of the invasion forces. He and two other soldiers were assigned to guard bridges in Normandy. On June 9, three days after the D-Day invasion, Private Van Laningham was killed in an air raid as German bombers flew over the region where he was working. He was a native of Mattoon and had worked at Kuehne Manufacturing. He enlisted in the army on March 19, 1942, and was shipped overseas on September 4, 1943, arriving in England.

Like many war veterans Private Van Laningham was buried near where he was killed, and his body was not returned until after the war. His body was returned in 1948, and a funeral with full military honors was held at Schilling Funeral Home on Sunday, May 9. A visitation was held at the home of his parents, Mr. and Mrs. Leon Van Laningham, 800 N. 30th Street. Private Van Laningham was survived by his parents and two brothers.

In 1959 Private Van Laningham's parents sold three acres of land next to their home on 30th Street to the city of Mattoon for $4900 for the construction of a park. City Commissioner Elmer Goetz said the city had wanted to add a park on the northwest part of town, and he hoped there would be playground equipment and baseball fields ready the following summer. On Sunday, July 3, 1960, a ceremony was held to dedicate the new park.

This memorial sits on the far east side of the cemetery next to the grave of the unknown Confederate soldier. The old Mattoon High School building that sat near the corner of Western Avenue and 21st Street (which in later years was the old Central Junior High School) was torn down in 2006. 1946 MHS graduate Henry Bell was saddened to see his old school gone, so he decided to build a memorial as a tribute to all students who attended school there.

This monument sat in the middle of the memorial. A green and gold fence surrounded the memorial, and the names of MHS alumni who fought in WWII were printed on a sign behind the monument. Mr. Bell wanted the memorial to be a lasting tribute to all students and veterans from the old high school. At some point in time the fence and the wall with the veterans' names have been removed. All that currently stands is the monument.

Elmer L Ballinger SF 3/C
1912-1945

     Navy Shipfitter Third Class Elmer Ballinger was killed in action during WWII, but I was unable to find any information concerning the details surrounding his death. There were no articles from 1945 detailing what happened. I could also find no obituary. The only information I found was from a 1949 article that reported about his body being returned to Mattoon from overseas for burial.

     Mr. Ballinger was born in Mattoon and attended school here until his family moved to Terre Haute where he graduated from Gerstmeyer Technical High School. He married Loraine Cavolt. Mr. Ballinger entered the navy October 25, 1943, and was sent to Camp Perry, VA for training. He served in the Pacific for a year before being killed on April 28, 1945. He was survived by his parents and his wife.

Paul "Red" Graham
1920-1965
State Senator of Illinois 1960-1965

Paul Graham, a Mattoon native, was a State Senator when he died at the age of 45. Mr. Graham had been involved in politics at various levels for a number of years. He had served a term as chairman of the Coles County Board of Supervisors representing Mattoon Township, and was also a past school board member and Republican party precinct committeeman. He served one term in the Illinois House of Representatives before being elected to the senate in 1960. He was reelected in a landslide in 1964.

Mr. Graham was described as a "rotund man with red hair and an outgoing personality." Many accolades poured out after his death as there appears to have been a great deal of respect for him both as a legislator and as a person. He attended Eastern Illinois University for three years before joining the US Army Air Corps during WWII. Mr. Graham was a WWII combat veteran having served in Europe as an aerial engineer on a B-26 bomber. He compiled over 1700 hours of flying time during the war. Mr. Graham was co-owner, along with his father, of W.C. Graham and Son Auto Agency until the dealership was sold to Mattoon Imperial Motors in 1962. He also did work in public relations and as an insurance broker.

Early in 1965 Mr. Graham was diagnosed with colon cancer and underwent two surgeries at the Mayo Clinic in Minnesota. His condition was aggravated by anemia and he suffered a stroke on May 30. He passed away on June 18, less than five months after his cancer diagnosis. His funeral was held at the First Methodist Church with military rites performed by the American Legion and the VFW. Mr. Graham lived at 116 Wabash Ave. He was survived by his wife, Virginia, and two sons, Michael and William who were still at home.

In 1967 the Little League baseball diamond at Lawson Park was officially named Graham Field in his honor. A memorial at the field, made of stone with a bronze relief of Mr. Graham, was dedicated at a ceremony on June 28. Mr. Graham had been a big supporter of youth sports, and he helped form the Little League organization in Mattoon. Members of Boy Scout Troop 57 conducted a flag raising ceremony at the dedication, and players from the city's fourteen Little League teams were present in their uniforms. I have fond memories of having played Little League baseball on that very field as a kid. I suppose I always took for granted the work people like Mr. Graham did to make that league and those opportunities possible.

Graham Field monument at Lawson Park

Robert O. Block
Staff Sgt. 30 INF 3 DIV
World War II
Jan 20, 1915-Nov 10, 1943

Staff Sergeant Robert Block served in the infantry during WWII in both North Africa and Europe. He died in combat but had already esteemed himself as a hero before his death when he was awarded the Silver Star for bravery under fire. Sergeant Block graduated from Mattoon High School and worked for C.W. Harris. He entered the army in February 1941 and landed in North Africa November 8, 1942. He was killed in a battle at Mt. Rotunda, Italy, about 100 miles from

Rome. Sergeant Block's parents received a letter from one of his fellow soldiers, Corporal Thomas Johnson of Florida, who said he had seen Block get killed, and he had subsequently killed the German soldier who killed him.

A few weeks before he died, Sergeant Block was awarded the Silver Star for bravery under fire. The citation for the award read, "Showing outstanding initiative and courage, Sergeant Block disregarded intense enemy machine gun and machine pistol fire striking within two feet of him, to climb upon a stone wall and direct light mortar fire on a German counter-attack. His gallant action under direct enemy fire for about ten minutes allowed his mortar to knock out one enemy machine gun and at least two German pistol-men." Looking for another hero? Here he is. Sergeant Block graduated from Mattoon High School where he was a football star. His body was returned home in 1948, and a funeral was held at the Methodist Church with full military honors. He was survived by his parents, a brother and three sisters.

Robert D. Phipps
Feb 20, 1913-Aug 10, 1944
3rd INF DIV 30th REG
Killed in France

Private First Class Robert Phipps graduated from Mattoon High School where he was a star football and basketball player. He married Helen Butler and went to work for The Texas Company in Mattoon. He enlisted in the army in August 1943 and was sent overseas. He fought in Italy, taking part in the capture of Rome, and was then involved in the invasion of southern France.

I could find no articles that provided specific information about the circumstances surrounding Private Phipps' death. He was buried in the Draguisnan cemetery in France with full military honors and Catholic rites. A few weeks prior to his death Private Phipps was awarded the Combat Infantry Badge. Private Phipps' body was returned to Mattoon in 1948, and a funeral was held at the Church of the Immaculate Conception. Private Phipps was survived by his wife, a small son Robert, his father, five brothers and four sisters.

Jacob Berkowitz
June 7, 1906-Oct 27, 1985
City-Circuit Court Judge 1936-1976

Jacob Berkowitz was elected to a six-year term as a Judge of the Mattoon city court in 1936, replacing Judge C.H. Douglas. He received his commission in Springfield on Friday, February 7, 1936, from Governor Henry Horner. He would end his judicial career four decades later.

Jacob Berkowitz was born in Terre Haute, the youngest of ten children. In grade school he developed an interest in the law and knew from an early age that he wanted to be an attorney. He fulfilled that dream in 1931 when he graduated from the law school at the University of Illinois and passed the Illinois Bar. He went to work for the firm of Vause and Kiger in Mattoon.

After serving as a city judge in Mattoon, Berkowitz was appointed as an associate judge for the fifth circuit. He was elevated to circuit judge in 1971 and was elected chief judge of the Fifth Judicial Circuit in 1972 replacing Chief Judge Harry Hannah. These are impressive accomplishments under any circumstances, but even more so considering the fact that Judge Berkowitz lost his eyesight in 1952. After losing his sight, Judge Berkowitz relied on help from his wife who was a certified court reporter and from his secretary Marjorie Suddes. Both women read reports to him. Berkowitz was the first blind chief judge in the state.

Judge Berkowitz started a program in the fifth circuit where judges were assigned to conduct pre-trial hearings on all civil cases. This resulted in substantially fewer cases going to trial resulting in savings to taxpayers and litigants alike. While the practice is common today, it was groundbreaking at the time.

Jacob Berkowitz passed away at Barnes Hospital in Saint Louis at the age of 79. He was survived by his wife, Hazel, and two daughters.

WWI

Expeditionary Forces
In Memory of all Service Men
Who Fought and Died in Action
Post 4325

The American Expeditionary Forces (AEF) was the name given to the American troops serving in Europe during World War I. When Congress declared War on Germany in 1917, the United States did not have the organization necessary for the deployment of the enormous numbers that would be required.

On May 26, 1917, General John Pershing was instructed to take his staff to France. Shortly after arriving, Pershing cabled the War Department that he would require at least a million men by the following May and that there could be as many as three million eventually needed. In response to the German attacks in the spring and summer of 1918, Pershing placed the entire American forces at the disposal of the Allied high command, delaying until July the formation of the American First Army. Two divisions of Americans deployed near Paris at Chateau-Thierry stopped the German advance.

When the Armistice came, approximately two million American troops had been transported to Europe. By the end of August 1919, the last American division had set sail, leaving only a small force in occupied Germany. Pershing and his staff embarked for America on September 1, 1919.

Mattoon resident and WWI veteran John Hardwick purchased and donated this monument to honor all AEF veterans. Hardwick served in an army machine gun company during the war. The monument was officially dedicated at a 2:00 pm ceremony on Sunday, October 20, 1974. Retired army Colonel John Farrar spoke at the dedication, and the Rev. Roger Compton gave the invocation. The Mattoon High School band provided the music.

In Memory of Edwin C Elliott
S Sgt 57 Bomb Wing AAF
World War II
Jan 11, 1920-May 10, 1944

Edwin Elliott was born in Kentucky and moved with his family to Windsor where he grew up. His family moved to Mattoon where he completed his last two years of high school and was an outstanding student in the ROTC program. He was working at a gas station at the corner of Fourteenth Street and Broadway Avenue when he joined the army in October 1941. In November 1942 he was shipped overseas where he served in North Africa before being reassigned to Italy. On May 10, 1944, according to a telegram received by his parents, Sergeant Elliott was killed instantly during an airplane crash over Corsica, Italy.

Sergeant Elliott's plane, a B-25 bomber, went down for unknown reasons during a non-combat mission. His remains were not recovered which is why his stone reads "In memory of." However, over 60 years later a military research and recovery team was able to locate and identify his remains. Sergeant Elliott's body was returned to Mattoon where a funeral attended by his surviving relatives was held at the Mitchell-Jerdan Funeral Home on May 11, 2010. A graveside service with full military rites was conducted at the cemetery. Although Sergeant Elliott's memorial stone was placed in Dodge Grove at the time of his death, his physical remains were buried in Resthaven Memorial Gardens.

Grave marker at Resthaven where Sergeant Elliott's remains were buried

Owen L. Albright
PVT 83 ARMD RCN BN
World War II
October 3, 1918-August 28, 1944

Betty Albright, the wife of Army Private Owen Albright, received a telegram on August 28, 1944, that said her husband was missing in action. Owen Albright was working at Kuehne Manufacturing in Mattoon when he enlisted in the army in July 1941. Owen and Betty were married in July 1943, and he was shipped overseas in September. Two months after receiving word that her husband was missing Mrs. Albright was notified that he had been officially listed as killed in action. Private Albright had been sent to France two days after D-Day. Private Albright's body was returned home for burial on April 27, 1949. He was survived by his wife, parents and three sisters. I was unable to find any information about the circumstances surrounding his death.

William D. Hardin
TEC 4-16 INF
Oct 26, 1919-Nov 14, 1945
Bronze Star Medal

I was really curious about this tombstone. Obviously, Mr. Hardin was in the military. And being just twenty-six years old he had no doubt served in WWII, but the war was over by November 1945 so he would not have been killed in action. Was he still in the army? Had he been discharged and died back home in some kind of accident? A little research revealed a sad, and probably scandalous, scenario of the untimely death of a civilian just months after his discharge following a very heroic tour of duty.

Sergeant William Hardin spent 33 months in combat during WWII. During that time he fought in North Africa, Italy, Belgium and Germany. He also made amphibious landings in North Africa, Sicily and Normandy. During that time he earned eight major battle stars, the Combat Infantryman Badge, a Bronze Star, the French Croix de Guerre and two Presidential Citations. His war-time service was exemplary to say the least. In June 1945 Sergeant Hardin was discharged and returned home where he got a job with CIPS.

A little after 3:00 am on the morning of Wednesday, November 14, 1945, the Charleston Police Department received a call complaining that a car had been parked with its motor running for a substantial length of time in a residential area. Upon arrival officers found four occupants in the car. Three were dead and the fourth was rushed to the hospital in critical condition. Two of the dead were William Hardin and his twenty-two-year-old brother John of 620 Piatt Avenue in Mattoon. Mrs. Leo Millage of Charleston was also dead, and Mrs. Harold Reynolds was unconscious but still alive. One of the men and one of the women were in the front seat of the car, and the other couple was in the back seat. The husband of Mrs. Millage had returned home from overseas service two weeks earlier but had moved out after he and his wife got in a rift. Mrs. Reynolds' husband was in the army and was still overseas.

Coroner Horace V. Clark said the cause of death appeared to be carbon monoxide poisoning from gas generated in an old-fashioned heater in the car in which the victims were found.

Nathaniel Kention Moore
CPL-USMC
Nov 9, 1982-Jan 26, 2005
Fighting Terrorism in Iraq
"He Stayed the Course"

Corporal Nathaniel Moore was one of 31 Marines killed in Iraq when a helicopter crashed during a sandstorm. The crash occurred near the town of Rutbah, approximately 220 miles west of Baghdad. Corporal Moore's mother, Amber, is an animal control officer in Champaign where Nathaniel spent much of his childhood. She is well known among city employees who rallied around her. Champaign Police Deputy Chief John Murphy commented on the family atmosphere among the employees and said donations were being taken for the family. A scholarship in Nathaniel's name was started with the donations. It is set up to offer college scholarships to graduates of the Lincoln's Challenge Academy which Corporal Moore had attended.

Corporal Moore was born in Urbana, the son of Duane and Amber Moore. He was survived by his parents and a sister, Amanda. Given an inscription on the back of his stone and things I read, Nathaniel was very protective of his sister and the two had a very close bond. I can only imagine how proud she must be of her big brother, and rightfully so. He joined the Marine Corps after the 9/11 terrorist attacks, wanting to serve his country. He did so with the utmost integrity and bravery, and he died a hero.

134

Captain Judith L Decker
USAF
1942-1969

     Captain Judith Lynn Decker was a nurse in the US Air Force. She graduated from Mattoon High School in 1960 and from the Decatur School of Nursing in 1963. She joined the Air Force in January 1964 and was commissioned as a Second Lieutenant. She was stationed in Japan for over two years then served a tour in Vietnam. After that she was transferred to a base in Thailand. Captain Decker was found dead in her quarters at the age of 27. The cause of death was listed as pulmonary congestion and edema.

     Captain Decker was survived by her father, Melvin Decker, a sister Darla who was a student at Eastern Illinois University, and three brothers. She was posthumously awarded the Air Force Commendation Medal.

135

Robert Carew
Born May 7, 1861 Waterford Ireland
Died Sep 9, 1926 Ranger, Texas

Here's a man who was born in Ireland the year the US Civil War broke out, died in Texas and was buried in Mattoon. I found this all very interesting and was curious to learn more about this man. A handful of articles in the local paper gave a glimpse into Mr. Carew's life, but I couldn't find anything that told how or why he ended up in Mattoon from Ireland.

Robert Carew was a retired conductor for the Wabash Railroad and had lived in Mattoon for several years. He never married and had no family in the United States. At some point in time he had moved to Desdemona, Texas, and was taken to Ranger, Texas, for treatment after falling ill. He passed away after two months in Ranger.

Mack Sparks of Mattoon, an old friend of Carew's, notified another of their friends, W.E. Butler of Los Angeles, who went to Ranger and was with Carew when he died. Mr. Butler accompanied his friend's body to Mattoon for burial, then returned to Texas to help settle his estate.

Mr. Carew had three brothers. One was a retired British Navy Captain who lost a leg and an arm in WWI. He was operating the Hotel Sinai in a city on the Suez Canal in Egypt. Another brother was a retired British Army General living somewhere in England, and the whereabouts of the third brother were unknown.

136

The large mausoleum is probably the most recognizable feature in Dodge Grove cemetery. It is a beautiful structure with a grand appearance. Above the main door is an inscription that reads, "They rest from their labors. Their works do follow them." I was curious about the structure's history. Who built it? How was it funded? How old is it?

An advertisement in the *Journal Gazette* dated January 8, 1913, gave a glimpse of what was to come as it described the future structure which was in the planning stages. The ad begins, "Have you ever stood with bared head in the rain or snow at the side of a friend or relative and experienced the disagreeable sensation of having the final ceremonies over the body of the deceased conducted under circumstances most disagreeable and dismal?" It goes on to explain that you could ensure future ceremonies will take place in "a magnificent marble chapel in a light warm room, without haste, in a dry room shielded from the weather." The final pitch read, "In this modern method of interment the remains are fittingly entombed in an adjoining room, not an arm's length away, and we are comforted by the thought that no king or queen of old or ruler of modern times has had any more fitting burial place than the one which a few dollars, by our foresight, have thus provided." For further information, the reader could call or write the Mattoon Mausoleum Company, Office Number 6 Demaree Building, Phone 668.

The mausoleum company paid the city $3000 for the building site, and they established a perpetual care fund. The building was constructed of concrete and Indiana limestone. It took a near direct hit from the 1917 tornado but sustained only minor damage. The mausoleum was dedicated on Sunday, June 28, 1914.

In 1962 an organization called the Crypt Owners Association took over the mausoleum from the Chicago ownership. The association had been formed fifteen years earlier to assist with maintenance of the building which had been neglected. Of the 320 crypts in the mausoleum at the time, 75 remained unsold. The association's goal was to sell the remaining crypts and to use the funds for care and maintenance of the building. H.R. Checkley of Mattoon served as president of the association.

By 1986 there appears to have still been an issue with there being no money for upkeep and with the building continuing to deteriorate. The city of Mattoon purchased the mausoleum for $7727. Mattoon resident Martha Morgan was credited with spearheading an effort to tend to the building. Her parents are interred there, and she began to question its state of disrepair. City building inspector Don Brigham said there were still several crypts available, and he hoped they could be sold to raise money for repairs. Mayor Roger Dettro said the first tasks would be to sandblast and tuckpoint the building's exterior and fix the leaking roof. Once that work was done, the mayor was hopeful funds would be available to do some inside work.

The first person interred in the mausoleum was 16-month-old Howard M. Jones on March 26, 1913. The last person who was interred in the mausoleum was Vivian Petrovich who was placed there on June 9, 2014. Spaces are still for sale and can be purchased from the city. Members of the public can enter the mausoleum on Memorial Day each year when it is unlocked. Other than that it is kept locked to prevent unauthorized access, vandalism, etc. Family members of those who are interred have their own key.

Veterans who served in multiple wars and/or earned multiple medals

Morgan Phipps, WWII, Korea

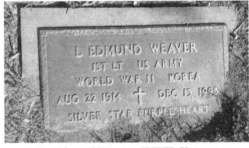

L. Edmund Weaver, WWII, Korea

Ernest Albert Stevens, WWII, Korea, Vietnam

Delbert D Diepholz, Bronze Star, Purple Heart

138

John D Stoltenberg, Korea, Vietnam

Guy O Petty, Bronze Star, Purple Heart

Thomas Earl Miller Jr., WWII, Korea

Francis M Yarbrough, WWII, Korea

CL Harris, Purple Heart, Victory Medal

Arnold A Park, WWII, Korea, Vietnam

Marvin R Tilford, WWII, Korea

Albert C Huckaba, WWI, WWII

139

Kenneth R Seaman, Bronze Star, Purple Heart

Harold A Lidster, WWII, Korea

Leo Sylvester Jobe, WWI, WWII

Joseph J Thompson, Korea, Vietnam, PH, Bronze Star

Jack J Kimrey, WWII, Korea

William A Louthan, WWII, Korea

Joseph A Matthews, Bronze Star, Purple Heart

Kenneth D Heckler, WWII, Korea

Lovell A Neal, WWI, WWII

Willard Shelton, WWII, Korea, Vietnam

George Ray Morrison, WWII, Vietnam

Alvin L Phillips, WWII, Korea

Dale F Harper, WWII, Korea

William W Daugherty, WWII, Korea

Carol Gwyn Rosaire, WWI, WWII

Wayne E Shadwick, WWII, Korea

Harold M Millar, WWII, Korea

Raymond L Cardinal, WWII, Korea

Robert Wendell Jackson, WWII, Korea

R L Tucker, WWII, Korea

Wayne Morris Gardner, WWII, Korea

George W Perry, WWII, Korea

Imogene L Simpson, WWII, Korea, Vietnam

Charles E Petrie, Korea, Vietnam

Richard D Kendrick, WWII, Korea, Vietnam

Wilbur L Smith, WWII, Korea, Vietnam

James Robert Fairchild, WWII, Korea, Vietnam

Lionel M Homan, WWII, Korea, Vietnam

Joe Mitchell, Bronze Star, Purple Heart   Vert Enis Jr., Bronze Star, Purple Heart

Jonas F Bontrager, WWII, Korea

Veterans of the Spanish-American War

I wanted to recognize veterans of the Spanish-American war because it tends to be one of those forgotten wars, and because there appear to be few veterans of that war compared to others. It took place in 1898 sandwiched in history between the Civil War and WWI.

The Spanish-American War was a conflict between the United States and Spain that ended Spanish colonial rule in the Americas and resulted in U.S. acquisition of territories in the western Pacific and Latin America. The war originated in the Cuban struggle for independence from Spain, which began in February 1895. The Cuban conflict was bad for U.S. investments in the island, which were estimated at $50 million, and almost ended U.S. trade with Cuban ports, normally valued at $100 million annually.

In addition to U.S. monetary interests there was an appeal to American humanitarian sentiment. Under the Spanish commander, Capt. Gen. Valeriano Weyler y Nicolau, nicknamed "the Butcher", Cubans were herded into so-called "reconcentration areas" in and around the larger cities, and those who remained at large were treated as enemies. Spanish authorities made no adequate provision for shelter, food, sanitation, or medical care, and thousands died from exposure, hunger, and disease. These conditions were graphically portrayed for the U.S. public by sensational newspapers, notably Joseph Pulitzer's *New York World* and William Randolph Hearst's recently founded *New York Journal*.

The popular demand for intervention to stop the war and assure Cuban independence gained support in the U.S. Congress, but the expression of congressional opinion was ignored by

144

President Grover Cleveland, who opposed intervention. His successor, William McKinley, was equally determined to preserve peace with Spain, but, in his first instructions to the new minister to Spain, Stewart L. Woodford, and again in his first message to Congress, he made it plain that the U.S. could not stand by and see the bloody struggle drag on indefinitely.

Riots in Havana in December led to the sending of the battleship *Maine* to that city's port as a precaution for the safety of U.S. citizens and property. On February 9, 1898, the *New York Journal* printed a private letter from the Spanish minister in Washington, Enrique Dupuy de Lôme, describing McKinley as "weak and a popularity-hunter" and raising doubt about Spain's good faith in her reform program. De Lôme immediately resigned, and the Spanish government tendered an apology. The sensation caused by this incident was eclipsed dramatically six days later. On the night of February 15, a mighty explosion sank the *Maine* at her Havana anchorage, and more than 260 of her crew were killed. Responsibility for the disaster was never determined. A U.S. naval board found convincing evidence that an initial explosion outside the hull (presumably from a mine or torpedo) had touched off the battleship's forward magazine. The Spanish government offered to submit the question of its responsibility to arbitration, but the U.S. public, prompted by the *New York Journal* and other sensational papers, held Spain unquestionably responsible. "Remember the Maine, to hell with Spain!" became a popular rallying cry.

The demand for intervention became strong in Congress by both republicans and democrats and in the country at large. U.S. business interests, in general, opposed intervention and war, but that opposition diminished after a speech in the Senate on March 17 by Senator Redfield Proctor of Vermont, who had just returned from a tour of Cuba. Proctor described his observations of the war-torn island: the suffering and death in the reconcentration areas, the devastation elsewhere, and the evident inability of the Spanish to crush the rebellion. His speech, as *The Wall Street Journal* remarked on March 19, "converted a great many people on Wall Street." Religious leaders contributed to the clamor for intervention, framing it as a religious and humanitarian duty. Diplomatic efforts were tried and failed, and Congress declared war on Spain on April 25, 1898.

A two-front war was waged in Cuba and in the Philippines. While the American army was a formidable force, it was the overwhelming naval superiority that left no doubt the war would be quick and would result in a decisive American victory. In fact, the war would conclude just four months after it began in August 1898.

Spain had nothing to match the four new battleships, *Indiana*, *Iowa*, *Massachusetts*, and *Oregon*, which formed the backbone of the North Atlantic Squadron, and in the Philippines the cruisers of Commodore George Dewey proved equally superior. Thanks largely to the energy and enthusiasm of the assistant secretary of the navy, Theodore Roosevelt, the U.S. ships had engaged in battle maneuvers and target practice and were well supplied with fuel and ammunition. Officers and men were confident and aggressive, whereas their Spanish opponents knew they were doomed to defeat.

Armistice negotiations conducted in Washington ended with the signing of a protocol on August 12, 1898. Besides ending hostilities, this agreement pledged Spain to surrender all authority over Cuba and to cede Puerto Rico and an unnamed island in the Mariana Islands to the

145

United States. In the Philippines, Spain consented that the United States should occupy the city and harbor of Manila until the conclusion of a peace treaty that would determine the final disposition of the islands. 385 Americans died in combat and another 1600 died due to disease. Eleven American soldiers were captured as prisoners of war.

George W Robinson

Charles Holland Shutts

Howard S Lytle

Edward O Henneke

Marcus L Carruthers

Raymond Coon

Charles E Rudy

Justin Hughes

William C Herring

Edward Ashworth

George P Giebler

Calvary Cemetery

The Catholic Parish in Mattoon was established in 1856, but they did not have a cemetery until 1881. Father John Crowe, pastor of the Church of the Immaculate Conception at the time, purchased approximately twenty acres of land on the north end of town between 16th and 19th streets for use as a cemetery.

A legend I found in a centennial book the Parish had printed in 1984 told of a Mrs. George (Jane) Russell who lived in the 900 block of Broadway. After attending one of the first funerals in the new Calvary Cemetery she said she wouldn't bury her dog in such a place. A short time later, on March 16, 1881, her husband died and was buried there.

Major improvements to the cemetery were undertaken in the 1920s. The cemetery was under the control of a cemetery board and the church trustees. Daniel Burtschi served as Parish Business Manager until 1925 and was instrumental in the development of the cemetery. John Goetz served as the first superintendent of the cemetery. It was during the period of leadership of Mr. Burtschi and Mr. Goetz that the grounds were plotted and improved and perpetual care initiated.

In 1983 and 1984 major improvements were made to Calvary Cemetery. The gray polished granite entry on N. 19th Street replaced the old block pillars that had stood since the 1920s. The entry was a gift in memory of the Hoag family. The roadway was also widened and new landscaping was installed.

148

The Cox Children: Gary, Mary, Theresa, E. Louis, Kenneth

On April 27, 1968, the most famous and brutal crime in the history of Coles County was committed northwest of Mattoon, the senseless murder of five children of William and Lydia Cox. The children were Kenneth, age 5, Gary, age 7, Katherine, age 8, Theresa, age 9 and Edward Louis, age 16.

Eighteen-year-old Mattoon High School senior Thomas Charles Fuller lived with his parents and a sister at 2716 Marshall Avenue. He was dating Louise Cox, age 16, a junior. On the day of the murders Fuller was visiting with Louise at her family's home northwest of Mattoon. Fuller arrived at the home around 11:00 am. Mr. Cox was out of town, and Mrs. Cox left the house to take her daughter Patty to the hospital for treatment of a burn on her hand. Louise would later recall that when Fuller arrived at the home he was "calm and normal." Louise had prepared some pie as a snack, and while the children were eating, her brother Louie asked Fuller to go outside and do some target shooting. They left the house, and a few minutes later Gary and Kenneth finished eating and went outside to join them. The girls were already outside playing.

Louise would testify at a later hearing that after about 15-20 minutes Fuller returned to the house for a drink of water. She asked where Louis was, and Fuller said, "out back." He went back outside and returned a short time later for another drink. This time he said he had shot some birds and went back outside. When he returned to the house the third time, he asked Marie Cline, a family friend who was at the house, for a ride back to town. Before leaving, Fuller didn't kiss Louise or tell her goodbye. She would comment that both of those were unusual and strange. After Fuller left the house Louise went to look for her siblings and found her slain sisters in a corn crib behind the house. The bodies of her dead brothers were found nearby.

There are various theories about the motive for the killings. Fuller was known to resent the amount of time Louise had to spend watching after her siblings and he wanted to "free her" of the obligation so she could spend more time with him, and possibly run away with him. Louise also acknowledged that there were hard feelings after her father denied Fuller permission to marry her. A few months prior Fuller had proposed to Louise, and he asked for her father's permission to marry. Mr. Cox said no because he felt Fuller was too young and had no means to support her. Louise also mentioned an incident the day of the murders that angered Fuller. She had been

149

involved in an argument with her three brothers, and they had pulled her hair and hit her. She cried out to Fuller for help, and he was angry at the boys.

What is not in dispute is that Fuller murdered the five children by shooting each one with a .22 pistol. One child died of a single gunshot wound, the others were shot multiple times. The killings were senseless, barbaric and unprovoked. Fuller was spotted the next day in Charleston and was arrested without incident. The murder weapon was still in his possession. Fuller later pled guilty to the murders and was sentenced to two consecutive sentences of 70-99 years.

In an interview years later a family friend would recount many of the difficult things the family faced beyond the tragedy itself. For example, she noted the logistical challenges of the funeral, needing to find five hearses and 30 pallbearers. The Cox family vacated the home never to return again. Two days after the funeral Mr. Cox was quoted in the paper as saying the family was looking for a house to rent. "I can't say I'll never drive by there. That place did hold a lot of wonderful memories." He said friends had suggested taking a trip to get away, but they decided not to. He said, "I talked to my wife and we decided all we can do is brace up and face it here. All our friends are here. No matter where we go we can't get away from it." Seven children survived, including Louise. Mrs. Cox passed away in 2006, and Mr. Cox passed away in 2010. I can't imagine the pain of losing one child let alone five.

As of this writing Fuller is still incarcerated at the state prison in Hillsboro. He has never expressed any remorse, even going so far as to blame the Cox family and to say hateful things about them. In September 2019, the 69-year-old murderer had his 17th parole hearing which was denied by an 8-5 vote of the prisoner review board. Apparently nearly half of the board's members believe there is an amount of time an inmate without remorse can serve to pay for taking the life of five innocent children. Fuller is eligible for another parole hearing in September 2020.

Sgt. Scott B. Stream
March 4, 1969-Feb 24, 2009
US Army
Iraq, Afghanistan

Sergeant Scott Stream was a National Guard soldier attached to Co. B, 2nd BN, 130th Infantry in Effingham, IL. Pushing 40, the veteran soldier had already completed service in Iraq when he was deployed to Afghanistan. He was considered an "old-timer" whom the younger soldiers looked up to. On February 24, 2009, Sergeant Stream was one of two Illinois National Guard soldiers killed when a vehicle they were in was blown up by a roadside bomb.

By all accounts Sergeant Stream was a man who put the needs of others above himself. One example of this occurred in December 2008. Sergeant Stream was in Afghanistan and received a slot to return home on leave to spend Christmas with his family, his wife Rasa and their two daughters. He gave that slot to a young soldier who was homesick. Sergeant Stream told his colleague he could go home for Christmas and he (Stream) would take his leave in March and go home for his daughter's birthday. Sadly, he never made it home alive.

Sergeant Scott Stream was a man who knew and lived the meaning of sacrifice and service. This memorial stone was placed in his honor in Calvary cemetery while his remains were buried in the Kentucky Veteran's Cemetery in Hopkinsville, KY where he was originally from.

Louis F Mayer Jr.
T Sgt US Army Air Corps
World War II
Mar 24, 1921-Jan 3, 2005
Prisoner of War

Louis Mayer grew up at 3224 Richmond Ave. As a child he was a newspaper carrier, and he later worked for the Sally Ann bakery in Mattoon. He enlisted in the US Army Air Force in January 1942, one month after the Japanese bombing of Pearl Harbor. In April of that year he was home on furlough following his training before being shipped overseas. He was assigned to the North African command and flew missions over Italy.

Louis Mayer was promoted to the rank of Staff Sergeant and was an engineer and wing gunner on a B-17 bomber, also known as the Flying Fortress. In September 1943, just five months

151

after his family had seen him when he was home on leave, they received word that he had been reported as missing in action. Two weeks later Sergeant Mayer's family received word that his plane had been shot down over Italy, and he was being held by the Italians as a prisoner of war. Two of the plane's engines were destroyed by enemy fire, and the plane went down in the sea near Salerno. They were informed by the Red Cross that they could write to him care of Italian Camp No. 54, Military Post 3300.

Approximately two weeks after being captured, Sergeant Mayer escaped from the Italian POW camp with two other members of his crew. They were hidden by an Italian family for five months working in an olive orchard wearing civilian clothes. Their uniforms, which had been left in a barn, were discovered by German soldiers, and they were recaptured and nearly executed as spies. Sergeant Mayer and his colleagues were sent to Stalag VII-A in Munich, then to another POW camp where they were imprisoned until near the end of the war.

When the Russian army was so close they could hear their mortar fire, the German guards rounded up the prisoners and marched them nearly 500 miles, eventually passing through Berlin. Rations of bread and water were doled out, and the prisoners were beaten on multiple occasions for trying to take food from gardens. The prisoners were finally liberated by Allied troops on May 2, 1945.

Sergeant Mayer received a Presidential Citation, Air Medal with three oak leaf clusters, European-African-Middle Eastern medal with three battle stars and a Purple Heart. Mr. Mayer passed away on Monday, January 3, 2005, at Sarah Bush Lincoln Health Center. He was a retired accountant with Albright Equipment Company. He was survived by his wife, Betty, two sons and a daughter.

Thomas L. Grissom
Sept 22, 1956-Aug 16, 2002
American Youth Baseball
Hall of Fame Umpire
Cooperstown, NY
August 2001

Mattoon resident Tom Grissom was a softball and baseball umpire who reached the pinnacle of any professional in the sport of baseball, enshrinement in the National Hall of Fame in Cooperstown. Mr. Grissom had been a baseball and softball umpire for 31 years. He had umpired in all 50 states and in 21 foreign countries. Mr. Grissom participated in a parade in Cooperstown for the inductees, and he received a Hall of Fame ring. In addition to his recognition as a baseball umpire, Mr. Grissom is also a member of the Mattoon Softball Association Hall of Fame as an umpire.

Mr. Grissom passed away on Friday, August 16, 2002, following a three year battle with cancer. Even while battling cancer he continued to umpire. He was a Navy veteran and had worked at Vesuvius in Charleston. Mr. Grissom was survived by his wife, Kathleen, two sons and two daughters.

In Memory of Our Son
William V. Bergfeld EM 1/C
Dec 30, 1922-Nov 7, 1944
Lost at Sea U.S.S. Growler

The *USS Growler* (SS-215) was actually the third ship of the United States Navy named for the growler, a fish commonly known as large mouth bass. She was launched on November 2, 1941, and the submarine and her crew performed admirably in ten combat patrols between then and September 1944. *Growler's* 11th and final war patrol began on October 20, 1944, in a wolf pack with *Hake* (SS-256) and *Hardhead* (SS-365). On November 8 the wolf pack, headed by *Growler*, closed a convoy for attack, with *Growler* on the opposite side of the enemy from *Hake* and *Hardhead*. The order to commence attacking was the last communication ever received from *Growler*. After the attack was underway, *Hake* and *Hardhead* heard what sounded like a torpedo explosion and then a series of depth charges on *Growler's* side of the convoy, and then nothing.

All efforts to contact *Growler* for the next three days proved futile. The submarine was listed as lost in action against the enemy, cause unknown. During her first ten patrols *Growler* sank 17 enemy ships.

Electrician's Mate Second Class William Bergfeld was born in Effingham and moved with his family to Mattoon when he was in grade school. He attended St. Joseph's parochial school and Mattoon High School. He enlisted in the navy in January 1941 and served thirteen months on the aircraft carrier *USS Saratoga*. Bergfeld then attended submarine school in Connecticut and was assigned to the *Growler*. He was on board the sub when Commander Howard Gilmore ordered her submerged in enemy waters after an attack. Gilmore was injured and knew he was unable to get inside, but he ordered the sub submerged anyway sacrificing his own life for the safety of his crew. The sacrifice was regarded as one of the most heroic actions of WWII, and Commander Gilmore was posthumously awarded the Congressional Medal of Honor.

Neither the *Growler* nor any of her crew members were ever recovered. A memorial service was held for Mr. Bergfeld on Monday, December 31, 1945, at the Church of the Immaculate Conception. He was survived by his parents and four brothers.

Lt. John Mullaney
June 19, 1923-Sep 23, 1950
Killed in Korea

I couldn't find any articles that provided information about the specifics surrounding Lieutenant Mullaney's death. I was also unable to locate his obituary. From a handful of snippets I came across I was able to piece together some information about him. Lieutenant Mullaney had served in WWII in Italy, Sicily and Northern France and must have performed heroically because he was awarded both a Bronze and Silver Star. He was killed in action just 23 days after arriving in Korea. Lieutenant Mullaney and his brother, Walter, were co-owners of the Ricky movie Theater at 2921 Shelby Ave. He was survived by his wife Martha who later remarried.

Lt. Edward Ritter Jr., USN (MC)
July 12, 1909-Oct. 23, 1944
Lost in China Sea

Navy Lieutenant Edward Ritter was a doctor who served in the naval medical corps during WWII. He was born in Mattoon and graduated from Mattoon High School in 1927. He graduated from Harvard University in 1931, and served as editor of the school newspaper, *The Harvard Crimson*. He then attended Northwestern University School of Medicine, graduating with an M.D. in 1937. His specialty was eye surgery.

After residencies and internships elsewhere, Dr. Ritter served at the Brooklyn Navy Hospital for a little over a year before being transferred to the Philippines. Following the outbreak of the war, he was reported as missing in action on April 12, 1942, while serving in Manila. He was later confirmed to be a prisoner of war at the Bilibid prison.

Lieutenant Ritter was declared lost in the sinking of a Japanese prison ship on October 24, 1944, per a telegram received by his parents, Mr. and Mrs. Edward Ritter Sr. of 2408 Western Ave. Apparently the ship, which was not marked as a prison transport ship, was sunk by Allied bombers. The cable received by Ritter's parents read, "On October 11, 1944, Lieutenant Ritter, who had been a captive in Bilibid prison camp in the Philippines, was placed on board a Japanese freighter, apparently enroute to Japan. The ship was anchored in the cove of an island about 200 to 300 miles from Manila for about six days before it returned to Manila on October 20 and from there in a convoy of Jap ships proceeded in a general northwest direction. On October 23 this ship, which bore no marks to indicate it was carrying prisoners of war, was torpedoed and sunk off Shoonan, eastern coast of China. Records maintained by the Japanese authorities in the Philippine Islands have come into the possession of the United States naval personnel and those records reveal that your son did not survive the sinking."

Lieutenant Ritter was survived by his parents and a brother, William.

As you enter Calvary Cemetery, straight ahead is a flagpole, a beautiful cross monument and a plaque that reads, "Prayerfully remember all veterans. In memory of SP4 Nicholas Thoele, Teutopolis, IL. 9/4/1950-5/24/1970." The cross monument is called the Crucifixion group. Daniel Burtschi had it imported from Italy and erected as a memorial to his family.

Nineteen-year-old Army Specialist Nicholas Thoele of Teutopolis was killed in action in Cambodia during the Vietnam War. His unit was on maneuvers in Cambodia when they encountered hostile enemy fire. Specialist Thoele was wounded and was placed on a medical helicopter for evacuation to a hospital. The ambulance helicopter was fired on and shot down, and Specialist Thoele was killed in the crash.

Specialist Thoele was a 1968 graduate of Teutopolis High School and worked at the Norge plant in Effingham before enlisting in the army. He was sent to Vietnam in September 1969. The memorial marker was dedicated in October 2018. Specialist Thoele was the brother of Marianna Hughes of Mattoon.

James William Sullivan
PVT US Army World War II
Jan 19, 1925-May 18, 2018
1974 Pulitzer Prize
Newsday

The Pulitzer Prize is an award for achievements in newspaper, magazine and online journalism, literature, and musical composition in the United States. It was established in 1917 by provisions in the will of Joseph Pulitzer, who had made his fortune as a newspaper publisher, and is administered by Columbia University. Prizes are awarded yearly in twenty-one categories. In twenty of the categories, each winner receives a certificate and a $15,000 cash award. The winner in the public service category is awarded a gold medal. As far as I can determine, Mr. Sullivan is the only Mattoon native ever to receive this distinguished award.

Mr. Sullivan earned the Pulitzer as a staff member of *Newsday* magazine for work he did investigating how heroin traveled from France to Long Island. The series was covered in a book called *The Heroin Trail*. Sullivan's investigative work for the story included going along with police as they used a battering ram to knock in a door during a drug raid. Mr. Sullivan thought highly of law enforcement and worked closely with them throughout his career.

In an interview with Rob Stroud of the *Journal-Gazette* after Mr. Sullivan died, his son Dennis said his father had wanted to be a reporter since he was in elementary school in Mattoon. An English teacher noticed he had writing ability and encouraged him to pursue his interests. He also worked in the industry as close as a child can, working as a newspaper carrier.

Mr. Sullivan moved with his family to Indianapolis where he graduated from high school. After graduation he enlisted in the army and served during WWII fighting in North Africa, Italy and Germany. He worked for several newspapers and did some freelance work for *Time* magazine. While working for *Time* he contributed to a cover story on race riots. He turned that work into a book he co-authored, *Race Riots New York 1964*.

Mr. Sullivan worked as a mid-level staffer on the senatorial campaign of Robert Kennedy. He retired from *Newsday* magazine in the 1980s as city editor.

Richard J. Goodwin
Illinois
SGT 1954 AACS SQ AF
Sept 17, 1931-Feb 1, 1952

Air Force Sergeant Richard Goodwin died at the age of 20 in 1952 during the Korean War. I assumed he had been killed in action. That appears not to have been the case, but the circumstances surrounding his death are somewhat unclear. A February 21, 1951, article said Goodwin was promoted to sergeant, his second promotion since arriving in Korea, so he did serve in that war. He enlisted in the Air Force in October 1948 and served as a radio operator. He arrived in Korea in December 1950.

On February 1, 1952, Sergeant Goodwin's parents, Mr. and Mrs. B.P. Goodwin of 812 N. 22nd Street, received word their son had died of asphyxiation at the Johnson Air Base near Tokyo, Japan. The telegram they received said a letter would follow with details of the circumstances surrounding his death. I couldn't find any follow-up articles that told what those circumstances were.

Sergeant Goodwin was born in Mattoon. He attended Lowell and Lincoln elementary schools, Longfellow Junior High and Mattoon High School. His body was shipped home, and a funeral was held on March 4, 1952. A graveside service was held with full military honors. One can only speculate why he was in Tokyo. Perhaps he was on leave. Perhaps he had ended his combat tour and was reassigned. Also, one can only speculate as to what exactly happened to cause his death. Sergeant Goodwin was survived by his parents and a grandmother.

Burrell P. Goodwin
Illinois
PFC 33 MIL POLICE CO
World War I
Aug. 17, 1899-Jan. 26, 1956

Burrell Goodwin, a veteran of WWI, is buried next to his son Richard. I had been curious about Richard's death when I suspected he may have been killed in action during the Korean War. When I saw Burrell's tombstone, I suspected he was Richard's father and my research later confirmed that he was. I was also interested in Burrell's story because he was, like me, a Military Policeman. I couldn't find any information about Burrell's war service, only mentions that he served in WWI, but nothing about when or where.

Burrell died at the age of 56, in January 1956, four years after his son died in Tokyo. He passed away at Memorial Hospital after a lengthy, unspecified, illness. Mr. Goodwin was born in Moultrie County. He worked for the Sally Ann Baking Company for 20 years before becoming a Metropolitan Life Insurance agent. His obituary said his only child, a son Richard, was accidentally killed in Japan in 1952. Burrell was survived by his wife Mary, four brothers and a sister.

Irish Immigrants

For as small as Calvary Cemetery is, there are a number of people who were born in Ireland. Several tombstones identify the deceased as having been born there, and I suspect there are others as well who didn't have that mentioned. It really isn't surprising to find this dynamic because there were large waves of Irish immigrants throughout the eighteenth through the twentieth centuries, and the majority of them were Catholic. It is well documented that a number of early Irish-Catholic immigrants settled in Illinois and established churches here.

Voluntary Irish immigration to America began with a small trickle of immigrants in the 1700s. In 1695 stringent anti-Catholic laws were introduced, and by the early 1700s Irish Catholics held just seven percent of land in Ireland. British laws prevented Catholics from freely immigrating to America. Irish immigrants during the 1700s were, therefore, mostly Presbyterians from the north of Ireland, who are referred to as "Scots-Irish." Many of the Anti-Catholic Laws were repealed in the 1790s, and Catholic Irish were able to immigrate to America. Irish immigration to America significantly increased in the early 1800s, inspired by the American ideals of "Life, Liberty and the pursuit of Happiness". Shipping company agents placed immigration advertisements in Irish newspapers and journals. Posters were displayed in Irish towns and villages. Irish immigrants in the early 1800s undertook the voyage on sailing ships which took up to three months. Immigrants left from ports all over Ireland including Derry, Cork, Limerick and Galway. Many were offered free passage from Ireland to Liverpool where the majority of ships bound for America started their voyage.

Irish immigration to America in the 1800s rocketed as Ireland was devastated by the Irish Potato Famine in the 1840s. The devastation of the Irish Potato Famine is hard to imagine. People were faced with death by starvation. Thousands of men, women and children resembled skeletons with wasted limbs and emaciated faces. The Irish Potato Famine led to associated diseases such as typhus and dysentery. The Famine was made even worse by unusually harsh weather conditions as Ireland was subjected to bitter cold gales of snow, sleet and hail. Many felt the only escape was to immigrate to America. During the period of the Irish Potato Famine, between 1845 and 1849, the population of Ireland dropped from 8 million to 6 million due to death from starvation or emigration. In the 1840s, the immigrants from Ireland constituted nearly half of all immigrants to the United States.

Irish immigrants migrated into Illinois in greater numbers after the state opened to settlement in the early 1820s. If there was a job in building a railroad, or even a road like the National Road, the Irish were willing to work. During the 1830s, rivermen, tradesmen and craftsmen developed a strong Irish presence in Cairo. Some places in Illinois, like Tipperary town in Monroe County, were named after Irish counties where most of the residents were from. Tipperary town was the first of many towns where the Irish built upon their religious beliefs. St. Patrick's Catholic church, the first Catholic church in Tipton, was erected in 1850.

The construction of the Illinois Central railroad also brought Irish immigrants. Advertisements in 1852 enticed Irishmen to "come forward and assist in laying this mighty track." Vandalia, Fayette County, and South Pass (Cobden) in Union County were locations of large labor camps. The influx of Irish workers to work on the railroads in Illinois is well documented, and it's not a stretch to assume at least some of the Irish citizens in the area that would become Mattoon came here seeking work with the railroad.

Obviously in the span of just a few paragraphs it is impossible to summarize all of the ins and outs of a topic as complex as centuries of Irish immigration to America and, more specifically, to central Illinois. I have tried, however, to provide a glimpse of how Mattoon came to be inhabited by so many Irish Catholics who made a life here and died and were buried here. Here are but a few of the tombstones I found in Calvary Cemetery that bear inscriptions indicating that the deceased was born in Ireland:

Maria Gorman, born August 25, 1869, Clonmore, Queens Co., Ireland

Mary O'Connor, born in 1800, Waterford, Ireland

Mary O'Connor, born in 1840, Waterford, Ireland

Edward Dunn, died in 1917, age 71, born in Longford, Ireland

John Montgomery, died in 1890, age 54, born in Inver, Co. Donecal, Ireland.

Edward Barrett, born in the County Cork, Ireland, April 18, 1900.

161

Daniel Shay, born in Co. Claire, Ireland, December 25, 1919.

Raymond R. Raef
Illinois
PVT 483 ORD EVAC CO
World War II
Nov 11, 1908-July 28, 1944

Private Raymond Raef, age 36, was killed in action in France during WWII according to a telegram from the War Department that was received by his brother Urban Raef of 1817 Grant Ave. This news was printed in an article in the *Journal-Gazette* on August 21, 1944, about three weeks after he was killed. No details surrounding his death were reported, and I couldn't find any follow-up articles that had any.

Private Raef was born in Mattoon. He attended St. Joseph's parochial school and graduated from Mattoon High School. He worked for his brother as a sheet metal worker before joining the service in February 1940. He left for overseas duty in March 1944 and was with an armored evacuation company. He was survived by a son, Raymond, and a daughter, Joyce, both of Springfield, MO and by four brothers and two sisters.

Private Raef's body was shipped home in July 1949 after the war. A funeral was held on Saturday, July 9, 1949, at the Church of the Immaculate Conception under the auspices of the American Legion.

Horace A. Worland
Ensign U.S.N.R.
Mar 14, 1923-Jan 25, 1945

Twenty-one-year-old Horace Worland was an Ensign in the US Navy. He died in the Naval Hospital in Pensacola, FL from injuries sustained in an airplane crash. When his family received word of his death no details surrounding the circumstances of the crash were included.

Ensign Worland was born in Neoga but was raised in Mattoon. He attended St. Joseph's parochial school and was a graduate of Mattoon High School. In high school Horace was an excellent golfer having tied for the state championship his junior year and winning the Big 12 conference championship as a senior. When he graduated he was one of ten students honored for both academic and athletic ability.

Ensign Worland attended the Bradley Technical School in Peoria and the University of Illinois in Champaign before enlisting in the naval reserve in 1942. He was called to active duty September 1, 1943, and received training in Kentucky, Arkansas, Georgia and Texas. He was receiving the final phase of his training in Pensacola, FL and was due to earn his wings in March.

Ensign Worland's funeral was held Wednesday, January 31, 1945, with full military honors. He was survived by his parents, two brothers and three sisters.

Whitley
Kathy, Tommy, Norma
January 24, 1954

The thing that strikes you as you walk past this tombstone is that there are three children, ages 11, 9 and 2, buried here and they all died on the same date, January 24, 1954. If you're not familiar with the story, you can't help but wonder what tragedy came to this family.

In the early morning hours of that fateful day, just after midnight, a fire broke out at the home of Mr. and Mrs. Walter C. Whitley at 8 Noyes Court. An article in the next day's newspaper said the parents were not home when the fire broke out, but it didn't say where they were. It was reported that Mr. Whitley arrived home while rescue attempts were underway.

The following day it was reported that Fire Chief L.E. Weaver had requested assistance from the state fire marshal's office in investigating the cause of the fire. Chief Weaver was able to rule out a handful of possible causes on his own, however. For example, some neighbors had reported hearing an explosion. While the furnace in the basement appeared to be the possible ignition point, there was no damage to it that would indicate an explosion, and the furnace's electrical controls were found to be intact.

Firefighters found the clocks in the home to have stopped around 12:15, possibly due to electrical wiring burning and shorting out at that time. Testimony at a Coroner's inquest on January 27 shed more light on what happened. Chief Weaver and Firefighter Lawrence

Metzelaars both testified. Metzelaars testified that he took the body of the two-year-old boy from his bed approximately four minutes after he arrived on scene while Weaver and Firefighter Bryann McCoy recovered the bodies of the girls. Metzelaars climbed a ladder to reach and enter the boy's west upstairs bedroom window. He stumbled over the bed of fourteen-year-old Walter Whitley Jr., who had managed to escape from the house, before finding the baby in his crib.

Police Lieutenant Hobart Clark attempted to gain access to the girls' room but was hampered by smoke and intense heat. He was overcome with smoke inhalation and had to be hospitalized. Other firefighters who helped battle the fire and who attempted to rescue the children were Captain Mark McAndrew and firefighter Harry Sullan. Firefighters were forced to retreat to the basement and knock down the fire before they could gain access to the girls' bedroom where they were both found dead.

Clothing from a chute apparently fell on the furnace's pipe causing the blaze. Chief Weaver estimated the temperature in the furnace's smoke pipe to have been between 500 and 600 degrees, and the burning clothing caused excessive smoke. Another witness to testify was Janice Brown. She was babysitting at a nearby residence, and Walter Jr. ran to the house where she was after escaping from his burning home. She called the fire department at 12:21 am.

It appears the fire spread up the furnace pipe very rapidly and was extremely hot. Intense heat and smoke filled the house creating a death trap for the four Whitley children. Fortunately, Walter was big enough to get out of the house to safety. The sad reality is there is nothing he could have done to save any of his siblings, and they never had a chance. Lieutenant Clark and the firefighters who arrived at the scene did all they could, and their actions were nothing short of heroic, but sadly their efforts were too late.

I wondered whatever happened to Walter Whitley Jr. I couldn't find much about him in the years after the fire, but I did find a 1963 article that told of him being recently commissioned as a Second Lieutenant with the Air Force after graduating from officer's training at Lackland Air Force Base in Texas. He was a graduate of Eastern Illinois University. His parents had moved to a home at 409 Crestview. A May 1964 newspaper announcement reported that Walter, now a First Lieutenant, was engaged to Diana Williamson of Mt. Prospect.

This beautiful monument is in honor of military veterans. The inscription on the main body of the monument reads, "Let this monument stand in honor and remembrance of those who lie in repose within Calvary Cemetery's hallowed grounds whom have served God and this great nation." The inscription at the base reads, "Dedicated to the memory of Anthony V. Sheehan II who loved God and country."

Kenneth J. Roetker
Illinois
PVT 117 INF 30 INF DIV
World War II
May 29, 1924-July 25, 1944

Private Kenneth Roetker was killed in action during WWII, but I couldn't find any specific information about the circumstances of his death. He was killed in action at St. Lo, France, according to word received by his wife, Rose Marie, of 808 Lincoln Ave. He had an infant daughter, Brenda Kay, when he died.

Private Roetker's body was shipped home in October 1948 for burial. A funeral with full military honors was held on Saturday, October 30, 1948, at the Church of the Immaculate Conception with the Rev. Father Daniel Daly officiating. Private Roetker worked at the Atlas Imperial Diesel Engine Plant in Mattoon before enlisting in the army. In March 1943 he took his basic training in North Carolina and was sent overseas on May 10, 1944. He had been overseas approximately three months before he was killed. He was survived by his parents, three brothers and his daughter. His wife remarried after his death.

Earl J. Sieben
Illinois
Staff SGT 324 INF 44 DIV
World War II
Feb 5, 1923-April 17, 1945

In July 1944 Army Private First Class Earl Sieben and Barbara Boggs, both from Mattoon, were married in Salina, Kansas, where Sieben was stationed. Barbara had worked in a local notion store in Mattoon, and Earl had attended the Charleston Teacher's College before he enlisted in the army. Less than a year later Sieben, then a Staff Sergeant, would be killed in action in WWII.

Sergeant Sieben was born in Humboldt and attended Mattoon schools. He graduated from Mattoon High School in 1941. He received his basic training at Fort Riley, Kansas, and was sent overseas in September 1944. None of the newspaper articles that reported on Sergeant Sieben's death provided any specific details. He was an infantryman serving with the 7th Army and was killed in action in Germany.

Sergeant Sieben's body was shipped home after the war. A funeral with military rites, including a firing squad and color guard, was held on Saturday, August 13, 1949, at the Church of the Immaculate Conception. Sergeant Sieben was survived by his wife, parents, a brother and two sisters.

Veterans who fought in multiple wars and/or earned multiple medals and veterans of the Spanish American War

George J Bruner, WWII, Korea

Thomas W Marti, WWII, Korea, Vietnam

Raymond E Hoelscher, WWII, Korea

James E Clodfelder, WWII, Korea, PH

Perry C Miller

Resthaven Cemetery

     Resthaven Memorial Gardens opened in 1936. It is and always has been privately owned. The current owners are Mark, Jim and Tom Bautista of Chicago. The cemetery's first owner, B.T. Atkins, wanted it to be called a memorial garden, meaning all the markers would be flat rather than raised. That policy changed several years ago, and a new section was opened that is devoted to upright markers.

     Tom Carver worked at Resthaven for 50 years and his son, Mike Carver, took over from him. Mike worked many summers with his father and feels like he grew up here. Mike's son, also named Mike, works for the cemetery now.

     Resthaven has seen many changes over the years. An east entrance, something Tom Carver wanted for a long time, was finally added several years ago. Another change occurred in the early 1960s when Interstate-57 came through. The interstate, which now runs along the western property line, is on land that once was owned by Resthaven. Three acres of Resthaven property that had not yet been used for burials was sold to the government for the project. The cemetery's maintenance buildings originally sat where the interstate is now.

Gordon Waymoth
MM2 US Navy
World War II, Korea
June 24, 1920-Jan 15, 1984

It's hard to make it out in the picture, but the medallion on this stone says, "Pearl Harbor Survivor's Association." I was really intrigued by this, because I hadn't come across any other stones indicating the deceased was a Pearl Harbor survivor. I've found a handful who were at Normandy on D-Day, who were prisoners of war and who died on navy vessels on the open seas, but none who were at Pearl Harbor.

Unfortunately, I couldn't find any articles that provided any information about Mr. Waymoth's service on that day. His obituary simply said he was a WWII veteran, he had eighteen years of service in the navy and he was on duty at Pearl Harbor when it was bombed by the Japanese. There were no articles in the archives that documented where he was, whether he was on board a ship or any other information.

I narrowed a newspaper archive search down to the years 1941-1946 hoping there would be an article detailing what happened to him either during the war or shortly thereafter when he returned home, but there were no hits on his name during that time frame. All that is known is that he was in fact a survivor of the attack on Pearl Harbor. Mr. Waymoth was survived by his wife, Eveline, and two sons who lived out of state.

Darrell E. Wehmeyer
1927-1991

The medallion on Mr. Wehmeyer's stone indicates he was in the US Maritime Service, more commonly known as the Merchant Marines. It has been called the forgotten service. In 1938, when a second World War was imminent the military realized that winning a war would require many ships to carry war supplies to the fronts. President Franklin D. Roosevelt ordered mass-production of Liberty ships and established the U.S. Maritime Service (USMS) to train the men needed to operate these ships. Joseph P. Kennedy, (father of President John F. Kennedy) was appointed as the first Chairman of the new Federal Maritime Commission in 1937, and he laid the groundwork for the U.S. Merchant Marine.

From July 1, 1941, to March 1, 1942, jurisdiction was under the U.S. Maritime Commission. From February 28, 1942, the U. S. Coast Guard, under Executive Order 9083, administered the training under the direction of the U.S. Maritime Commission. In July 11, 1942, Presidential Executive Order 9198 transferred operation of the Maritime Service to the War Shipping Administration. The USMS was first established under the Coast Guard and later supervised by U.S. Navy officers. Many of its first recruits in 1938 were from the Civilian Conservation Corps (CCC).

Men, caught up in the patriotic fervor of the time, came forward to serve in the fledgling U.S. Maritime Service. There were 37 Official U.S. Government Recruiting Offices set up around the country. Radio and newspaper ads brought in the thousands of young patriotic men, as young as 16 years of age, from every state who answered their country's call to serve. Mr. Wehmeyer is the only person I've come across who served in the USMS. There may have been others, but if so, they didn't have anything on their tombstone to indicate it.

A search of the archives revealed a handful of articles that indicate Mr. Wehmeyer was a very interesting person. The plane on his tombstone indicates he obviously loved flying. His obituary said he taught ground and instrument training at Lake Land College, and he was a retired pilot for Brit Airways. He also retired from CIPS as an automotive supervisor. In addition to serving in the Merchant Marines he also served in the Coast Guard.

I found an interesting article from 1966 that told of a heroic act Mr. Wehmeyer was involved in on December 8 of that year. He and a CIPS co-worker, Bill Foltz, rescued a man named James Godfrey of Litchfield from a rain swollen creek near Litchfield. Godfrey's car had washed over a bridge into a swirling creek after stalling on the bridge. He remained in the car until water rose up to his neck. He then climbed onto his car's roof and was swept away through a culvert about 500 feet downstream where he grabbed a tree limb, held on and began yelling for help. The creek was 40 feet across and was 12-14 feet deep due to the rain.

Mr. Wehmeyer heard Godfrey's cries for help, and he radioed in to Foltz and another employee named C. Flowers. Foltz and Flowers grabbed a boat from a yard in Nokomis and got oars from a local store, then rushed to the scene. Wehmeyer and Foltz manned the boat while Flowers held a rope that was tethered to the boat. The rope was too short, however, so Flowers released it. The boat capsized, throwing Wehmeyer and Foltz into the water. They managed to get to Godfrey and somehow pull him to safety. Godfrey was taken by ambulance to a doctor's office where he was treated and released. The only casualty was Godfrey's collie dog who drowned. The boat was recovered downstream. Godfrey's car was salvaged but was a total loss. It was two hours from the time when Godfrey's car was first swept off the bridge until he was pulled to safety.

Mr. Wehmeyer was survived by a son and four daughters.

James Walter Priest
PFC 7 CAV (INF) 1 CAV DIV (INF)
Korea PH
May 11, 1931-Aug 30, 1950

Private First Class James Priest was killed in action in the Korean War. Sadly, his parents did not know his fate until a few months after he was killed. PFC Priest joined the army October 8, 1948. On August 11, 1950, he phoned his family and told them he was being shipped to Korea.

It was the last they would ever hear from him, and in January 1951 they learned he had been dead since August.

PFC Priest had been in action less than a week before he was killed. In early January 1951 PFC Priest's parents, Mr. and Mrs. Walter Priest of 109 Richmond, asked the Red Cross for help in determining the whereabouts of their son. After nearly five months of waiting without news of their son, they received a telegram informing them of his death.

Mr. Priest attended Grant Park and Longfellow grade schools and Mattoon High School. He was survived by his parents, two brothers and two sisters. Several years later his brother Jack would serve in the Vietnam War.

Peter Lynn Rankin
CPL TRP L 3SQ 14 ARMD CAV
June 1, 1949-July 9, 1968

When I saw Corporal Rankin's tombstone I assumed he had been killed in Vietnam. He was a few weeks shy of his nineteenth birthday and served in an armored cavalry unit during the height of the war. While he was stationed overseas he was in Germany, not Vietnam.

Corporal Rankin entered the army in June 1967. After his training he was sent to Germany, arriving in January 1968. He sustained injuries in a car accident on July 7, 1968, just six months after arriving in Germany. He died two days later in a hospital in Wiesbaden, Germany.

Corporal Rankin, the son of John Rankin of 2717 Moultrie and Jean Rankin of 2700 Pine, was a 1967 graduate of Mattoon High School. In addition to his parents he was survived by three brothers, two at home and one who was a Warrant Officer in the army stationed at Fort Wolters, Texas. One can imagine how happy Corporal Rankin's family must have been when they learned he would be stationed in Germany instead of being sent to Vietnam. It was probably an answer to prayer because he would be out of harm's way.

Corporal Rankin's funeral was held on July 17, 1968, at Mitchell-Jerdan Funeral Home. His burial at the cemetery was with full military honors.

Nelson Earl VanGundy
CPL CO K 3BN MAR DIV
Vietnam PH
Feb 12, 1944-June 9, 1965

Marine Corporal Nelson Earl VanGundy became the first casualty of the Vietnam War from Coles County when he was killed in action on June 9, 1965. Corporal VanGundy died from gunshot wounds to the chest while on patrol in the vicinity of Chu Loi. He enlisted in the Marine Corps in December 1961 and had been in Vietnam only two months before being killed. Prior to that he had been stationed in Okinawa.

Corporal VanGundy's body arrived in Mattoon, accompanied by a Marine escort, on the afternoon of Tuesday, June 15, 1965, via the New York Central Railroad. His funeral was held two days later at Mitchell-Jerdan Funeral Home with military rites performed at the burial. Corporal VanGundy was born in Ames, Iowa but had lived most of his life in and around Mattoon. He was survived by his parents, Mr. and Mrs. William VanGundy, three brothers and two sisters. He was a member of Central Community Church. Corporal VanGundy was posthumously awarded a Purple Heart.

On Veterans Day in 1965 a memorial was dedicated to Corporal VanGundy, and to all casualties of the Vietnam War, in Peterson Park in Mattoon. It consisted of a flagpole and a boulder with a plaque. The memorial, which sits just inside the west entrance near the Peterson House, still stands today. Congressmen William Springer and George Shipley spoke at the dedication.

The flagpole and plaque erected in Corporal VanGundy's honor at Peterson Park

William Bryan
PVT Battery B 4 BN 65 ARTY
Sept 2, 1951-May 19, 1969

    William Bryan, who died in 1969 at the age of 17, was in the army so I initially thought he may have died in Vietnam. He died in California, but I couldn't find much information about his death. His obituary reads in part, "Army PFC William James Bryan, son of Mrs. James Fuller of 520 N. 18th, died Tuesday morning at Fort MacArthur, California. Death was reportedly due to a gunshot wound. Further details were unavailable." Obviously, he died on an army base so it could have been due to a training accident or it could have been suicide or even murder. There were no follow-up articles. PFC Bryan was survived by his mother, step-father, two brothers and two sisters.

Robert Joe Overmyer
LCPL CO K 9 MAR DIV
Vietnam PH
Sept 3, 1946-July 4, 1967

On the Fourth of July 1967, as Americans celebrated their freedom and independence, Marine Lance Corporal Robert Overmyer was literally giving his life to defend it in Vietnam. Mr. and Mrs. Lloyd Overmyer of 812 S. 33rd received word that their son had been killed in action after sustaining a head wound. No specific information regarding the circumstances was provided.

Corporal Overmyer was a 1964 graduate of Mattoon High School where he was a varsity letter winner in wrestling. He enrolled at Eastern Illinois University after high school and was majoring in zoology. He had completed two years of college before enlisting in the Marine Corps. He was a newspaper boy for several years and had also been employed two summers with the township park board.

The funeral for Corporal Overmyer was held on Wednesday, July 19, 1967, at the Church of the Immaculate Conception. Full military rites were conducted at the graveside by a Marine color guard and firing squad. Corporal Overmyer was posthumously awarded the Purple Heart.

Corporal Overmyer was survived by his parents and seven brothers and sisters.

Paul S. Mitskoff
US Merchant Marine
World War II
Nov 29, 1920-Nov 16, 1997

I had walked through all of Dodge Grove and Calvary cemeteries and not seen any graves where the deceased was identified as a member of the Merchant Marines. Then I saw the grave of Darrell Wehmeyer in Resthaven, and he was the first. Just a couple days later I saw this grave and learned there was a second Merchant Marine veteran buried locally.

I wasn't able to find much information about Mr. Mitskoff and literally nothing about his service during WWII. His obituary said he was living in Charleston, SC when he passed away, and he died in Summerville, SC. He married Jean Bullock of Charleston in 1976. She survived him.

In Memory of John Claire Sheridan
PHM2 US Navy
World War II
Mar 1, 1923-Dec 11, 1944

Pharmacist's Mate Second Class John Claire "Jack" Sheridan was killed in WWII when the ship he was serving on was bombed and sunk in the Pacific Ocean. Mr. Sheridan was a crew member on a destroyer that was escorting landing boats to Leyte on December 11, 1944, when his ship took three direct hits from enemy fire. The ship was reported to have blown up and sunk within two minutes. While some crew members survived, there were heavy casualties. Mr. Sheridan was initially listed as missing in action, but his status was changed to killed in action the following month.

Jack Sheridan was born in Clinton, IL and his family moved to Mattoon when he was two. He was a 1942 graduate of Mattoon High School where he was a member of the football team. He joined the navy in December 1942. In December 1943 he was sent overseas where he was stationed in New Guinea before being assigned to the destroyer in July 1944. Mr. Sheridan was survived by his parents and a brother, Navy Lieutenant Donald Sheridan who was serving in India.

Marty W. Pattin
1943-2018

Marty Pattin is probably the most successful athlete ever to come from Coles County. Following high school and college where he was a star baseball player, Mr. Pattin went on to a thirteen-year career as a pitcher in the major leagues that included an All-Star appearance and pitching in the World Series.

Mr. Pattin was born and raised in Charleston where he began playing baseball in Little League. He was an outstanding player in high school and was a successful pitcher for Eastern Illinois University, where he attained a bachelor's and master's degree in Industrial Technology.

He was drafted by the California Angels in 1965 and went on to pitch for the Seattle Pilots in 1969 (which became the Milwaukee Brewers in 1970), and was named to the All-Star team in 1971. At the end of the season he was traded to the Boston Red Sox and in 1974 was traded to the Kansas City Royals where he would finish out his career as a starting and relief pitcher. Mr. Pattin pitched his final game for the Royals in the 1980 World Series.

After his playing career ended, he became the head baseball coach at the University of Kansas in 1982. Throughout his career he enjoyed many accomplishments and successes, but he was most proud of those close to home. He was proud to be inducted into the EIU Hall of Fame, but perhaps was most proud when the Charleston High School baseball field was renamed the Marty Pattin Field in his honor.

Mr. Pattin was preceded in death by his wife Vera who passed away in 1996. He was survived by two sons and six grandchildren.

The sign marking Marty Pattin Field at Charleston High School

Carol J. Specht
June 7, 1939-June 7, 1983

Mrs. Specht's grave is about as inconspicuous as it can be. You would certainly never walk past it and have any idea how she died if you weren't familiar with the story. Carol Specht was murdered in a brutal and senseless attack during the early morning hours of June 7 (her birthday), 1983. Most people who lived in Mattoon at the time will recall the murder. I was in the army stationed in Germany at the time, but I subscribed to the paper and had it sent overseas to me. I recall the shock I felt when I read about it because Carol's daughter Connie, who was my age in school, was also injured. I never knew Carol, but I can tell you Connie was as sweet a person as you could ever meet.

Mrs. Specht was a pension administrator for Massachusetts Mutual Insurance Company, but she was known in the community for her volunteer work that focused on, ironically, violence against women. She was a member of WAR (Women Against Rape) and CADV (Coalition Against Domestic Violence). Despite some initial speculation, her murder had nothing to do with her involvement in those organizations. The attack was random, and her killer (I refuse to mention his name) knew nothing about her.

Carol and Connie lived together in an apartment in Mattoon. Connie was 20 at the time and was a student at Eastern Illinois University. Carol had told friends about incidents of window-peeping in recent months. Just after midnight on the date of the murder the attacker broke into the apartment. He had a fetish for women's shoes and he was there to burglarize shoes from the apartment.

Connie had returned home around 9:00 pm the previous evening after visiting friends and went to her room to listen to music. She left her room at 11:30, saw her mother asleep on a couch in the living room and went to bed. Sometime later a noise woke Connie, and she saw a man in her room. Before leaving the apartment the man cut Connie's throat. She survived and would later testify against him at trial. Carol was stabbed six times and died of her wounds.

Carol's murderer was sentenced to death. He successfully lobbied the courts for another sentencing, but before that could happen then Governor George Ryan abolished the death penalty in Illinois. The killer was subsequently sentenced to life in prison. I have no idea what happened to Connie after the trial or where she ended up. I hope she was able to move on and find happiness in life. She deserves it.

In addition to Connie, Mrs. Specht was survived by another daughter, Margo Christian, of Charleston.

Eloise Piper Mattoon
May 23, 1921-July 9, 2015

Obviously, I was curious when I saw this tombstone. Mattoon is not a common surname, even in this community that is named after someone with that name. Mrs. Mattoon passed away at the age of 94 at Hilltop Nursing Center in Charleston. She was born in Sumner, Illinois, and married Hubert Mattoon there in 1946. Hubert was a great-grandson of this city's founder.

Mattoon was officially named in 1861 after William B. Mattoon, the chief construction engineer working for the Terre Haute and Alton Railroad and partner of the Massachusetts firm, Phelps, Mattoon, and Barnes. The reason for the honor is a little unclear. The most popular explanation in local lore is that he beat other claimants in a game of poker and named the town after himself. Others have contended he earned the naming rights because his rail crew arrived first or that residents hoped the wealthy Mattoon would invest in the town if they named it after him. Regardless, what is not in dispute is that the city was named for William Mattoon. And the wife of one of his great-grandchildren is buried in Resthaven.

Mrs. Mattoon retired in 1980 as a secretary at Kankakee State Hospital. She was a member of the Eastern Star, Daughters of the American Revolution and the First United Methodist Church. She was an avid bowler who traveled to compete in tournaments. She was also an avid Illinois basketball fan and rarely missed a game.

Mrs. Mattoon's husband preceded her in death. She was survived by a son and a daughter.

Robert G Babb
CPL US Marine Corps
World War II
June 20, 1925-Feb 8, 2007
Served on USS Minneapolis

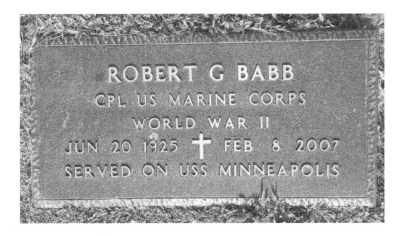

The *Minneapolis* was a naval warship that saw considerable action in WWII. It has a very interesting history, and it was involved in nearly every major engagement in the Pacific Theatre. It's no wonder why Corporal Robert Babb wanted to memorialize the fact that he had served on her during the war. I also learned that Mr. Babb, whom I had never heard of, was quite an interesting person. The kind of guy you would have loved to sit down with over a cup of coffee and listen to him tell stories. But first a little information about the *USS Minneapolis*.

The *USS Minneapolis* was commissioned in May of 1934 and made ready for service. She operated throughout Europe from July through September of 1934. After some additional work at her home shipyard, she was relocated to the west coast of the United States by way of the Panama Canal. She arrived in San Diego, California, on April 18th, 1935, and was subsequently assigned to the Cruiser Division 7. From there, she was given peacetime patrolling assignments along the American coast, made a side trip to Caribbean waters in 1939, and, in response to increased tensions with the Japanese, made her new home at Pearl Harbor, Hawaii, in 1940.

On the morning of December 7th, 1941, forces of the Imperial Japanese Navy struck military targets throughout the harbor. The end result netted the sinking or destruction of eight battleships, three cruisers, four destroyers, a seaplane tender, target ship, repair ship, tug and drydock Number 2. Fortunately for the *USS Minneapolis* and her crew, she had been sent off for gunnery practice and found herself some 20 miles from the harbor during the attack. Of all days to have left port for a routine training exercise, that piece of fate saved the *Minneapolis* and her crew.

Following the December events, the *Minneapolis* was refitted and sent on active patrols throughout the following January. She was later added to the carrier task force that included the *USS Lexington* and aided in the upcoming attacks on the Gilbert and Marshall Islands. During her early action, she recorded three confirmed aircraft kills while protecting the *Lexington*. From February into early March, *Minneapolis* opened her guns against Japanese shipping attempting to resupply the army garrisons at Gilbert and Marshall.

Her next prominent action found her fighting in the Battle of Coral Sea. The battle spanned from May 4th through May 8th and involved carrier battle groups from both sides. Once again, the *Minneapolis* was called on to protect the *Lexington* during the fight and once again she netted three enemy aircraft. However, the *USS Lexington* was severely crippled by two direct torpedo hits and an additional two dive bomb hits. *Minneapolis* sprang into action and rescued as many navy sailors as she could find. *Lexington* was sunk by the American destroyer *USS Phelps* to prevent her capture.

USS Minneapolis returned to action during the Battle of Midway. During three days in early June, she once again served as carrier protection. The battle netted some 250 enemy aircraft and, more importantly, four enemy aircraft carriers. *Minneapolis* played a critical role in defending the American carrier groups from enemy dive bombers and fighter harassment. She was then sent back to Pearl for resupply before rejoining the American carriers for their upcoming operations.

The Americans next took to invading Guadalcanal and Tulagi August 7th through the 9th. *USS Saratoga* suffered a torpedo hit by a Japanese submarine and was towed from the battle by the *Minneapolis* on August 30th. More landings followed and *Minneapolis* assisted in aerial defense as needed before being named flagship of Task Force 67, a cruiser-destroyer force designed to intercept enemy destroyers located off of Guadalcanal.

This narrative is just the beginning of the exploits of the *Minneapolis*. You could fill an entire book with information about the sea battles she engaged in. After the battle of Surigao Straight (October 24-25, 1944), the last major naval gunfire battle of the war and a decisive Allied victory, *Minneapolis* resumed her carrier protection duties and supported Allied landings where needed. She took part in actions at Luzon, Bataan, Corregidor and Okinawa where she downed four more Japanese aircraft.

Needing refitting, the *Minneapolis* sailed for Bremerton in Washington. After repairs and replenishment (including new gun barrels), she was back on duty, this time in Subic Bay of the Philippines Islands. By this time, the atomic bombs had been dropped on Hiroshima and Nagasaki and Japan officially surrendered. The official Japanese surrender of Korea to the *Minneapolis* occurred on September 9th, 1945.

So now a little information about Corporal Babb who served on this great battleship. He attended grade school in Sullivan, IL where he was a member of a basketball team that finished second place in state. His family moved to Murphysboro, IL where he graduated from high school in 1943. While in high school he earned varsity letters in football, basketball and track. He received a football scholarship to the University of Illinois, but was there only eight weeks before being inducted into the Marine Corps. Following his military service he enrolled at Eastern Illinois University where he lettered in football and track. In 1946 he recorded the NCAA's longest punt of 92 yards.

After graduation Mr. Babb accepted a position with USI Chemical company in Tuscola. In 1966 he was transferred to their plant in Xenia, Ohio, where he retired in 1987 as plant manager.

While in Xenia he was active in the community, serving as president of the Rotary Club and president and board member of the chamber of commerce. He was also elected to two terms on the Xenia city council.

Mr. Babb died at Sarah Bush Lincoln Health Center at the age of 81 and was survived by his wife of 59 years, Daisy, a daughter, two sons and several grandchildren. From comments in his obituary it appears that none of his personal achievements meant anything to him compared to his family.

Resthaven Monuments

There are a handful of monuments in Resthaven Cemetery. One, a memorial to members of the Masonic Lodge, was erected privately by the Masons. The others were added over time by the cemetery.

Stone carving of The Last Supper

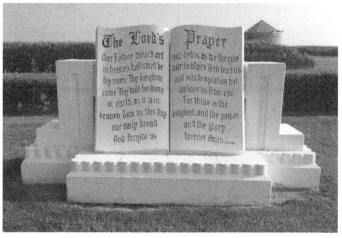

The Bible, opened to The Lord's Prayer

Masonic Memorial

This monument, a memorial to all veterans, sits at the far west end of the property

Veterans who served in multiple wars and/or received multiple medals

Dale D Burris Sr., Korea, Vietnam, Persian Gulf

James David Bolin, Purple Heart, Silver Star

Clarence A Bartels, Bronze Star, Purple Heart

Kenneth M Gray, Korea, Vietnam

William J McKinley, WWII, Korea

Walter I Kirby, WWII, Korea

Kenneth Edmond Perkins, WWII, Korea, Vietnam

Robert L Tweed, WWI, WWII

187

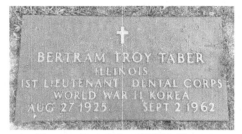

Bertram Troy Taber, WWII, Korea

Howard S Wyman, WWII, Korea

Jackie Lee Creek, Korea, Vietnam

Paul L Powell, WWII, Korea

Morris E Beals, Bronze Star, Purple Heart

Robert E Prince, WWII, Korea, Vietnam

Arthur L Kehrwald, WWI, WWII

Robert Brooks, WWI, WWII

Edward H Powers, WWII, Korea

James S Campbell, WWII, Korea

Riley C Klasing, Korea, Vietnam

Acknowledgements

With any project of this magnitude there is no way one can do it alone. I feel as though I have so many people to thank for helping me along the way. This project has taken months to complete. There were many days with hours spent walking cemeteries, then more hours, sometimes until late into the night, researching newspaper archives and internet sites digging for information. Then, of course, even more hours putting what I had found on paper. Or on laptop screen as the case may be.

First and foremost as always I owe a huge thanks to my family: my wife Kim and my daughters Katie and Rachel. I'm sure there were times when I seemed distracted and wasn't focused on other things like I should have been. I'm also sure there were times when they all listened to me drone on about some tidbit of information I had stumbled across. After many trips to one of the cemeteries I would come home and break into an impromptu history lecture about some person or event I had learned about. You know how it is when you're excited about something; you tend to go overboard with it, driving those around you nuts in the process. But they were all troopers and were supportive of this project.

I wanted to lead into each cemetery with a little background information about that particular cemetery. Dodge Grove was easy. There's a lot of information about it online, particularly on the City of Mattoon's website. There were, however, a few things I didn't know and a handful of things I knew were there but couldn't find. The sexton at Dodge Grove is Rob Newlin. Rob and I grew up together and he's been a friend since elementary school. I called him and told him what I was doing, and that I had some information I needed help tracking down. He said if I brought him a list of questions he would work on them. His assistance and knowledge were irreplaceable. Rob, thanks a million, buddy.

After I had moved on to Calvary Cemetery I searched online but couldn't find anything at all. I called my good friend Chris Considine who I know attends the Catholic Church and asked whether he knew anyone who might know the cemetery's history. He directed me to Phyllis Roytek and gave me her number. I believe Mrs. Roytek is in her 90s, and she is sharp as a whip. She is also very funny.

When I called her, she answered the phone, "Edgar County Sheriff's Department." I was confused and thought I had dialed the wrong number. After a little talking and explaining who I was, she revealed it was her. She laughed and explained that answering the phone that way throws spam callers off. That's the same kind of sarcastic sense of humor I have, and I fell in love with this woman immediately. Mrs. Roytek was very helpful in not only directing me to a resource that has a lot of the cemetery's history, but also sharing things with me that were recorded nowhere but in her mind. Phyllis, it was a pleasure visiting with you, and I greatly appreciate your help and expertise.

The resource Mrs. Roytek referred me to was a book that was published several years ago that is a history of the Mattoon Catholic Parish. I went to the Mattoon Library to see if they had a copy I could check out. When I walked in I was greeted by library director Carl Walworth. Carl took me downstairs and introduced me to Chris Suerdieck who volunteers in the library's local history center. Chris had a copy of the book, and he lent it to me. It had exactly what I needed. Thanks, Carl and Chris.

The last cemetery I walked was Resthaven. Like Calvary I didn't have much luck finding any information about that cemetery's history online. One day when I was out there I saw a gentleman weed-eating. I walked over, introduced myself and explained what I was doing. I asked whether he could help me find any information. The man's name was Mike Carver. He directed me to the office to speak with his father, Mike Carver Sr., who worked at Resthaven for 50 years. I walked to the office where I spoke with Mr. Carver and another employee, Angela Bradbury. They couldn't have been more friendly or helpful. Mr. Carver shared a great deal of information, and Mrs. Bradbury printed off some documents. I visited with them for at least a half hour, and they were very generous with their time. Mike Carver Jr., Mike Carver Sr. and Angela Bradbury, thank you!

Finally a big thanks to my editor and friend Beth Hauser. As always your advice and professional input was invaluable. I appreciate all you do. And I apologize for never getting straight when to use a semicolon instead of a comma, when to use whom instead of who and all that. In my defense I believe in the conspiracy theory cited by Creed on *The Office* who said, "Whom is a made-up word used to trick students."

Made in the USA
Monee, IL
01 April 2022

93964793R00109